BARRON'S

PAINLESS

Speaking

Mary Elizabeth, M.Ed.
Second Edition

To John H. Clarke,
who was there when some ideas began to grow
and who helped them on their way
—with my gratitude

All inquiries should be addressed to:
Barron's Educational Series, Inc.
250 Wireless Boulevard
Hauppauge, New York 11788
www.barronseduc.com

Library of Congress Control Number: 2011946121
ISBN: 978-1-4380-0003-9

PRINTED IN THE UNITED STATES OF AMERICA
9 8 7 6 5 4 3 2 1

BONUS MATERIAL

To access bonus materials, links
to speeches and other spoken
words you can hear online, and
other resources, visit the author's
Painless Speaking web page at:
http://www.edreinvented.com/products/painless-speaking/

ACKNOWLEDGMENTS

Appreciation goes to readers who commented on the manuscript, including Robert Hoberman, Marc Hull, Bernier Mayo, and Michael Podhaizer. Thanks to Ann Laberge and Dr. John Bisaccia for permission to use their writings. Special thanks to Xan Johnson for permission to use the scene from his play and for his assistance with preparation of sections of the manuscript related to his specialty of youth theatre.

The author gratefully acknowledges the following copyright holders for permission to reprint their work. And I gratefully acknowledge the contributions of my editor, Anthony Regolino.

Page 48: Diagram from "Semiotic and a Theory of Knowledge" from THE MESSAGE IN THE BOTTLE by Walker Percy. Copyright © 1975 by Walker Percy. Reprinted by permission of Farrar, Straus and Giroux, LLC.

Page 48: Diagram from "Semiotic and a Theory of Knowledge" by Walker Percy. Copyright © 1957 by Walker Percy. Copyright © renewed 1985 by Walker Percy. UK rights reprinted with permission of McIntosh & Otis, Inc.

Page 99: Program Cover: *The New Survivors: A Collage of Images from the Holocaust* by Keri Kunz, Copyright © 2002.

Pages 261–264: "Golf Fitness: What You Don't Know Might Hurt You" by Dr. John J. Bisaccia, Certified Sports Chiropractic Physician, Copyright © 2002.

Pages 265–267: "NELL'S KITTENS: An Analogy" by A. D. Laberge, Copyright © 2002.

Pages 268–274: A scored cutting taken from the script *The New Survivors: A Collage of Images from the Holocaust, Scene Two: Terezin—We Must Survive!* By Xan S. Johnson, Ph.D., Young Peoples' Theatre Specialist, University of Utah, Copyright © 2002.

CONTENTS

Chapter Five: Practicing and Performing "Think All You Speak" 205

Appendices 237

Index 276

INTRODUCTION

Speaking is only one of the communication skills that make up the language arts. For most people there are four main skills: **speaking**, **listening**, **writing**, and **reading**.* Speaking is closely related to these three other areas. Speaking and *writing* are alike in that they both express our thoughts to others. Speaking is understood by *listening*, and speakers must use listening skills themselves to judge how their words are being received. Speaking a text aloud (one way of *reading*) brings the receptive skill of interpreting written words together with the expressive skill of speaking. See how closely these skills are connected?

Lets take a moment to chart our course. Chapter One discusses the human voice and human language to help you understand the tools we have to work with in finding our voices.

Chapter Two defines one more essential term—the basic unit of speech communication, called an "utterance." Understanding what an utterance is helps us to understand how to be effective and considerate speakers. With that understanding, we can discuss one kind of speech we all use every day: conversation, the subject for the rest of the chapter. Chapter Two also covers guidelines and hints for face-to-face conversation, and conversations carried on using phone, e-mail, postal letters, instant messaging, SMS text messaging, tweets and direct messages, videochats and audiochats, and choosing between them. It also explores the difficult topic of negative conversation.

Chapter Three discusses reading aloud and oral interpretation—two special kinds of speaking that depend on a text. From an understanding of different kinds of texts, the chapter moves on to consider how texts make meaning and step-by-step preparation for reading aloud, plus hints for "cold" reading, if you have to read with little or no prep time.

Chapter Four teaches you how to compose a speech from the first steps right up to the finished product. Some people might think creating a speech is a writing process, but it is actually best done as an oral process, and you'll learn why in this chapter.

*Members of the Deaf community in America use American Sign Language (ASL) to communicate. In this book, we will refer occasionally to the communication skill of signing.

In Chapter Five you'll learn how to practice and perform speaking material, whether texts by someone else that you're reading aloud, prepared speeches, or speeches you have to give on the spot with little or no prep time.

When you're done, you'll have learned more about speaking casually and formally, about speaking with close friends and to audiences of people you don't know, about bringing to life the words of other people and words you wrote yourself, and about making up something effective right on the spot.

Henry David Thoreau says in his book *Walden,* "Could a greater miracle take place than for us to look through each other's eyes for an instant?" When we speak to others, we give them an opportunity to look through our eyes—we share our world with them, and open ourselves to their response. I hope that this book helps you to use your voice to truly connect to other people.

Speeches Online

There are some incredibly cool speeches available online, but remember that web addresses are constantly changing. Although the addresses provided were current when this book was written, sooner or later, some of the addresses may no longer work. If you should come across a web address (URL) that no longer appears to be valid, either because the site no longer exists or because the address has changed, either shorten the URL or do a keyword search on the subject matter or topic. Here's how:

- To shorten the URL, delete the end of the URL up to the first slash that appears after a three-character extension (typically .com/ .net/ .org/ .edu/ .gov/). This will usually get you to the home page of the website. From there, you may find a site map to help you, use a site search, or contact the webmaster to find out about the page you're looking for.

- To do a keyword search, type the phrase you're looking for with quotes around it into your favorite search engine. Many search engines list the top-rated sites first, so check the blurb about the top site, and if it seems good, try it out.

WARNING: Not every response to your search will match your criteria, and some sites may contain adult material. If you are ever in doubt, check with someone who can help you.

CHAPTER ONE

Finding Your Voice

ELEMENTS OF THE VOICE

You can probably recognize a number of sounds without any visual clues to help you. Voices of family members and close friends, singers in your favorite band, voices of cartoon characters like Homer Simpson and movie characters like Christian Bale's husky Batman, and the sounds of animals like cats and birds are typically easy to pick out. What's harder is trying to explain how we do it . . .

When we identify a sound or a voice, there are two reasons that it is typically difficult to describe the process. First, our recognition is usually just about instantaneous—we don't have to stop and think: we just know! Second, the vocabulary to describe the elements of the voice isn't often taught. But as we begin to study the art of speaking and learn to make conscious choices about how we use our voices, we need to know and name the elements that make up the sound of our voices to help us understand how we can use our voices more creatively and more effectively.

The elements of the voice have at least two functions. First, they communicate the meaning of what we're saying. Second, they also convey attitudes and emotions about both what we are saying and the conversation context. This addition of emotion and attitudes is a largely unconscious act that we need to make conscious in order to make effective use of our voices. To begin this process, let's introduce the eight elements of the voice.

EIGHT ELEMENTS OF THE VOICE	
Element	**Definition**
language	the string of distinctive verbal material that makes up what we say
pitch	how high or low our voice is
volume	how loud or soft our voice is
tempo	how quickly or slowly we produce sounds
tone	our attitude toward the content of what we're saying and toward our audience
stress	the amount of emphasis we place on each syllable
timbre	the personality in our voice
silence	pauses between sounds to breathe, create meaning, create rhythm, build suspense, etc.

All of these elements are involved every time we speak. The seven elements besides language are called **paralinguistic** elements or **paralanguage**.

Language refers to our pronunciation of the syllables that make up what we're saying in whatever language we're speaking. It also includes interrupters, like *ummm* and noises like *psst*. When we write down exactly what someone said, it is the word element that we are recording. Let's distinguish between *word* and *content*. The content is the meaning of the ideas or thoughts we express. The words are one way of conveying that content, but there could be other ways. Here's one way to think about the difference: When we *paraphrase* someone's words, we change the words but keep the content.

Pitch, volume, and **tempo** are pretty easy to understand: high/low; loud/soft; fast/slow. Some words that tell how people speak include the idea of pitch, like *squeak* and *growl*; some include volume, like *shout* and *whisper*, and some include tempo, like *babbled* and *drawled*. Some of the changes we make in these elements depend on content and some on conversation context. We speak at a higher pitch, more softly, and more slowly to babies. We also speak more slowly in formal situations.

Tone is most easily explained using an example. Imagine a line at a sports stadium for a tee-shirt giveaway. A little child is next in line when the last tee-shirt is given out and is clearly disappointed, but is given a shirt by the teen who was the last to receive one. The child's mother thanks the teen and says to her child, "Wow! Was that lucky!" enthusiastically and happily. The person behind her, who missed out on a tee-shirt says the same words "Wow! Was that lucky!" jealously. The difference is in the tone. Because tone is a challenging concept, here is a chart of different types of tone.

TONES OF VOICE			
General Categories	**Specific Tones**		
comic	amused	ironic	playful
	facetious	joking	satiric
	humorous	mocking	silly
instructional	critical	explanatory	thoughtful
persuasive	argumentative	coaxing	pleading
	believable	convincing	seductive

TONES OF VOICE, cont.			
General Categories	**Specific Tones**		
pleasant	approving	forgiving	peaceful
	calm	gentle	polite
	cheerful	gracious	sympathetic
	comforting	happy	tender
	compassionate	helpful	thoughtful
	content	joyful	tolerant
	courteous	kind	trusting
	elated	mild	
truthful	frank	innocent	sincere
unpleasant	accusatory	fierce	plaintive
	angry	flippant	pompous
	annoyed	frantic	querulous
	arrogant	frightened	reckless
	belittling	furious	regretful
	bitter	greedy	sarcastic
	boastful	grieving	saucy
	boorish	harsh	savage
	cocksure	hateful	scolding
	condescending	haughty	scornful
	contemptuous	horrified	servile
	crushed	hysterical	sorrowful
	defiant	impudent	spiteful
	desperate	insane	sullen
	disappointed	insulting	suspicious
	disgusted	intolerant	tragic
	dismal	irritable	uncomprehending
	domineering	jealous	uneasy
	egotistical	miserable	wild
	enraged	nervous	worried
	fearful	pitiless	
uninvolved	bored	languid	sluggish
	dull	monotonous	
	indifferent	nonchalant	

Stress is sometimes called *accent*, but we're going to avoid using that word because some people use *accent* to mean a "pronunciation of language by nonnative speakers or by native speakers from a different region than one's own." Stress is an important part of the pronunciation of individual words, as well as added to phrases to help convey meaning.

Timbre refers to the characteristics that make our voice uniquely ours, even when using the same sounds, volume, stress, pitch, tempo, tone, and silence as someone else.

Silence might be unexpected as a component of the voice, but speakers make unique uses of silence in between words. Silence includes pauses that occur for a variety of reasons. The great Russian acting teacher Constantin Stanislavski divided pauses into three types: breath pauses; logical pauses, dictated by meaning; and psychological pauses, used to convey the **subtext** of words.

Subtext is Stanislavski's name for "what lies behind and beneath the actual words," when feelings, thoughts, and imagination give life to "empty sound" so that "the word[s] become significant." (*Building a Character*, Routledge/Theatre Arts Books, 1977, p. 113). Here's an example. A friend could say "Look at my new netbook!" for a number of reasons, including:

- knowing you will be happy for him or her
- helping you decide about your upcoming netbook purchase
- showing off
- enticing someone talking to you to talk to him or her instead

That's the subtext, and it's often conveyed more by the other elements of speech, including the use of silence, than it is by the words.

As we study the elements of the voice, you'll discover that changing one or more of them, whether a little or a lot, changes how we sound and can even change what our words mean to others.

- A change in *pitch* can convert a statement into a question.
- A change in *tone*, from honesty to irony, for example, can make a statement mean its opposite.
- A quick, throwaway line that's amusing can become serious and heartfelt with changes in *tempo* and *stress*, so that it's said slowly with emphasis on each word.
- A statement that sounds calm at a moderate *volume* may sound threatening or aggressive if said at the top of one's voice.

But we are so used to making these adjustments in our voices unconsciously that, unless we make an effort, we probably aren't aware of most of the changes in the way we use our voices to make meaning. When we speak thoughtfully—and especially when we give vocal performances, such as acting in a play, reading a poem, or telling a story—we usually give the elements of our voices more thought and use more variety.

Trained professionals can do remarkable things with their voices. For example, an opera singer has to be able to express the most delicate and sensitive feelings—the type we associate with a soft and gentle voice—while singing loudly enough that the audience members in the last row can hear every syllable.

BRAIN TICKLERS
Set # 1

1. Each line of the chart asks you to read the following sentence in two contrasting ways. For each set of readings, note which elements of your voice you change, and how.

It's incredible! It's astonishing! Oh, it's unbelievable!

	First Reading	**Second Reading**
a.	as if scared	as if enthusiastic
b.	as if "it" is very likely unsafe, possible deadly	as if "it" is the fulfillment of your dearest wish
c.	as if you are becoming more and more convinced as you continue speaking	as if you are becoming less convinced as you keep speaking
d.	as if the person you are speaking to is approaching you from far away	as if the person you are trying to speak to is running away from you

2. Create a conversation in which you might logically say the following sentence: "We really ought to consider getting a pet orangutan." Experiment with the sentence until you find the intonation that makes you sound most convincing. Think particularly about which word you will stress the most.

(continued)

3. Read the Gettysburg Address on page 253. How would you read it if you wanted to move someone to tears? Describe your decision-making process. Be sure to mention the eight elements of the voice. Then tell the context in which you would choose to read the speech.

(Answers are on pages 40–42.)

Voice production

What actually happens when we speak? Well, there's a lot more to speaking than opening our lips and moving our mouths. Voice production coordinates our **breath production** with **vibration** and **resonation** and **articulation**. Here's how it works.

Voice production starts with inhaling. You may already know that our respiratory, or breathing, muscles—including the diaphragm and the intercostals, or rib muscles—help us to inhale and exhale air. After we inhale, the **excitors** (the respiratory or breathing muscles that regulate or control the supply of air that we need to produce our voices) gets voice production started.

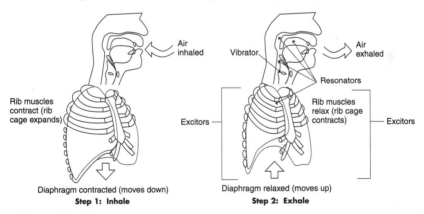

Step 1: Inhale — Rib muscles contract (rib cage expands), Air inhaled, Diaphragm contracted (moves down)

Step 2: Exhale — Vibrator, Air exhaled, Resonators, Rib muscles relax (rib cage contracts), Excitors, Diaphragm relaxed (moves up)

But we've all heard moving air—and it doesn't have the qualities of voice. How does it acquire these qualities? The air moves through a **vibrator**—our vocal cords, which produce sound waves when our breath travels across them. The sound waves are reinforced and amplified by **resonators** (the cavities of the chest, throat, mouth, and nose), which create the tone of the voice. The condition of these cavities affects how your voice sounds. If you have a stuffy nose, for example, the tone of your voice will be affected.

Now we have sound with tone, but this is not yet speech. We use the **articulators**—some of which are movable (lips, lower jaw, tongue, and soft palate) and some of which are not (teeth, upper gums, hard palate, and throat)—to shape each separate speech sound to create words.

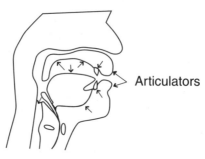

Articulators

You are probably familiar with all the articulators except, perhaps, the soft and hard palate. The hard palate is the top surface of your mouth, commonly called the "roof" of the mouth. The soft palate is behind the hard palate and is used to close the passage between the mouth and the nose. If you say "ng" repeatedly with a pause to exhale in between, you will feel the soft palate lower to allow air to go through your nose.

Fortunately, the vibrator and the resonators work involuntarily—we don't have to think about them. The excitors and the articulators, however, are under the speaker's control and need to be coordinated for speech to be understandable and effective.

BRAIN TICKLERS
Set # 2

Describe the process of voice production in your own words.

(Answers are on page 42.)

BEYOND LANGUAGE

Conversation means "an exchange of thoughts or words." At one time, if people said they were having a *conversation,* you would have assumed they were speaking in real time, either face-to-face or on the phone. With the development of new technology, more conversation contexts have developed. And due to cultural changes, interaction has come to be considered more important and is now invited in some situations in which communication used to be one-way. For example, have you noticed that news websites have added comment sections to every article?

Communication categories

As conversation contexts have multiplied, it has become more important to understand the different opportunities and restrictions that each context offers. All conversations, by definition, allow **verbal** communication, i.e., communication in the words of one or more languages, whether spoken, in text, or signed. But in many cases, one or more types of **nonverbal** communication (communication through means other than language) is or can be used, and when it is used, it is capable of enormous impact. Channels of nonverbal communication in conversations in which one sees and/or hears the other person include facial expressions, gaze, gestures, posture, touch, and use of personal space, as well as the paralinguistic elements of the voice. In other conversation contexts, you might find nonverbal elements such as **emoticons** like smiley faces, images, music, sound recordings, and video. Of course, there are some limitations: you can't include a video or sound file on a regular piece of paper in a letter sent via the postal service, but you can mail someone a CD or DVD with multimedia on it.

Nonverbal communication can have different roles, depending on what is being communicated, either confirming or disputing what is said in words. There are several reasons why verbal and nonverbal communication could be at odds. Sarcasm is a key situation. When a person speaks sarcastically or ironically, the literal words he or she says are frequently the exact opposite of what is meant. For example, someone might say, "Oh, yeah: he's a *great* friend" about a person who has failed to be a true friend. In our culture, we use tone of voice, emphasis, facial expression, and gestures to communicate the difference between the literal meaning of our words and our true attitude when we use irony or sarcasm.

Nonverbal and verbal messages can also be at odds if a person is concealing something, lying, or undergoing an internal conflict. For example, someone who finds a question or comment embarrassing or offensive may respond politely in words, but manifest discomfort nonverbally. Research into facial expressions by psychologist Paul Ekman formed the basis of the television series *Lie to Me*, which focused on a group of scientists using Ekman's techniques of analyzing **microexpressions**—involuntary facial expressions that signal anger, contempt, disgust, fear, happiness, sadness, and surprise and are difficult to fake—to uncover deception and expose people who were lying. In normal conversation, an alert conversation partner may notice these signs and gain understanding.

Two other communication categories have to do with conversational timing. People may participate in a conversation at the same time, called **synchronous** conversation, or at different times, called **asynchronous** conversation. The lag in asynchronous conversation may be any amount of time from seconds (with rapid text messaging) to weeks (with a postal letter sent from another country). The timing aspect of the conversation can have a variety of effects, for example, increasing anticipation for a reply, making communication more thoughtful, or tending to make people forget exactly where they were in their discussion. In the following chart Synchronous = S, Near Synchronous = NS, and Asynchronous = A.

DIFFERENT CONVERSATION CONTEXTS			
Form of Communication	**Synchronicity**	**Verbal Content**	**Nonverbal Content**
Face-to-face/F2F	S	✓	paralanguage, face, gesture, posture
Video Chat	S	✓	paralanguage, face
Phone Call	S	✓	paralanguage

DIFFERENT CONVERSATION CONTEXTS, cont.			
Form of Communication	Synchronicity	Verbal Content	Nonverbal Content
Instant Message/ IM (text)	S	✓	emoticons, file transfer
Phone Message	NS/A	✓	voice
Tweet; Direct Message	NS/A	✓	emoticons
SMS Text Message	NS/A	✓	emoticons
E-mail; MMS; Forum	NS/A	✓	emoticons, file transfer/ attachment
Website or Blog Comments	NS/A	✓	emoticons
USPS Letter (on paper)	A	✓	images, fonts
Magazine; Newspaper	A	✓	images, fonts

Differences in timing and nonverbal elements are significant. Perhaps the biggest differences are between seeing people or not seeing them as you converse and hearing their voices or not hearing them. Text—even packed with emoticons, images, and fonts that signal mood—has far fewer meaning clues than does a voice or a person who is present to you.

How to assess attitudes and emotions

One of the ways you can learn to be a good conversation partner and to gain mastery of your own speaking is to study how other speakers reveal attitudes and emotions. Of course, a person's **diction** or word choices may show emotion and attitude. Calling someone a *tightwad* rather than saying that he or she is *frugal* is an example of a revealing word choice: *frugal* is praise; *tightwad* is criticism. But even more may be learned from nonverbal clues. Paralanguage clues to look for include:

- changes in paralanguage elements during a conversation (for example, a change in tone or tempo);
- paralanguage elements that are different from the person's characteristic speech (for example, somebody who is usually boisterous being suddenly soft-spoken); and
- paralanguage at the extremes—very loud/soft/fast/slow/etc.

Body language is a term often used for nonverbal clues that aren't paralinguistic, and in this realm—which is mostly observed visually—you can look for these cues:

BODY LANGUAGE MEANINGS	
Element	**What to Look For**
facial expression	Alert and interested or uninterested and distant?
posture	Attentive or slumped?
gestures	Use of gestures usually indicates investment in what one is saying.
action	Repeated actions such as "bobbing" a foot or doodling can indicate lack of interest or preoccupation.
clothing/grooming	Not being dressed appropriately for an occasion can be a sign of lack of interest or disrespect.

Remember that we said that verbal and nonverbal communication don't always match up? When you begin to study how others express themselves using paralanguage and body language, you may begin to notice incongruities and discrepancies. Especially with people you know well, you may find that what the person claims to think or feel doesn't match what he or she says; what the person says doesn't match what he or she does; and/or that the person's words don't match his or her nonverbal communication.

in English, while *chien* means "dog" in French and *Hund* means "dog" in German. Knowing a language also means that you can create new sentences that you never heard before and figure out what is and isn't a proper sentence in your language.

What is dialect?

English is the native language of people from the USA, Canada, Britain, Ireland, India, Nigeria, Kenya, South Africa, the Bahamas, and Jamaica. If you've heard people from other countries speaking English, or even people from other regions of the United States, you've probably noticed some differences. One set of differences that distinguish English spoken in different places is called **dialect**. *Dialects* are mutually understandable forms of the same language that differ in systematic ways. Dialects develop when people who speak the same language are separated by geographical and social barriers. Changes in language develop slowly, and although differences give each dialect its own unique feel, mutual understanding is still possible. So people who speak American English and people who speak British English can have a conversation.

People who speak different dialects may have different pronunciations (**phonological differences**), but this is a feature of the dialect. Phonological differences connected to dialect are different from an **accent**, the word we will use to designate sound features of a person's native language that seep into his or her speech in a language he or she acquires later. Other differences between dialects include different words for the same thing (**lexical differences**), and word order differences (**syntactic differences**).

There is one dialect of English that many people talk about but nobody speaks. It is called Standard American English (SAE). According to Victoria Fromkin and Robert Rodman in *An Introduction to Language* (Harcourt Brace, 1998), SAE is "a dialect of English that many people almost speak. . . . SAE is an idealization. Nobody speaks this dialect; and if somebody did, we would not know it, because SAE is not defined precisely" (p. 408). African American English (AAE), on the other hand, is a dialect or group of dialects (including Black English and Ebonics), that is spoken by many African Americans who live in urban areas of the United States. Other dialects of English that are important in the United States are Latino English (spoken by immigrants from Spanish-speaking countries of South and Central America) and Chicano English (spoken by Mexican Americans in the Southwest and California), as well as regional dialects.

Dialects are suited for every kind of communication that a person needs to do. This is possible because within each dialect there are **styles** or **registers** that characterize how speakers of the dialect adapt their communications in more and less formal situations. Styles or registers are forms of speech that have developed to fit these different types of situations.

Just as there is a whole range of levels of formality in social situations, so there is in dialects. It's not as simple as "this word is formal; this word is informal." Nevertheless, we can broadly characterize the differences between formal and informal styles in English by noting some characteristic differences:

CHARACTERISTICS OF FORMAL AND INFORMAL STYLE IN AMERICAN ENGLISH	
Informal	**Formal**
contractions and abbreviations allowed	all words spelled out fully
slang, idioms, and colloquial terms allowed	standard forms and terms
fragments and run-on sentences allowed	standard sentence structure
fillers (*um*) and pauses allowed	clear, concise expression expected
taboo words allowed	euphemisms expected

ENGLISH FOR ALL OCCASIONS II: CULTURE AND ETIQUETTE

What is culture?

Not all differences in language use come from dialect. In his book *The Silent Language* (Anchor Books, 1981), Edward T. Hall, an American anthropologist, discusses **culture** as an essential element in all communication. Most culture is *acquired* rather than taught: we learn it by experience, not by studying it as a subject, so we are not consciously aware of it. This means that culture is like the lens of our eyes—it determines how we see, but we can never examine it fully ourselves because everything we see is seen *through* it. We can, however, make a purposeful effort to become consciously aware of our cultural assumptions. One way to do this is by making contact with another culture. Hall says that encountering another culture brings us into contact with "a completely different way of organizing life, of thinking, and of conceiving the underlying assumptions about the family and the state, the economic system, and even of mankind" (p. 23). Encountering another culture can make us aware that certain things that we took as givens were only cultural assumptions that we wouldn't have had if we had been born somewhere else.

Take time. Our ideas about time markedly influence our communication. In the United States, what we consider punctual is being no more than 3 to 4 minutes later than an agreed time, and we value punctuality highly. Other cultures don't place the same value on being punctual, not because they're lazy, slow, or uncaring, but because they have a different (and perfectly legitimate) understanding of time. Legitimate as it is, you can probably imagine that unless people are alert to the fact that their cultural lens is not "the right way," there will be major misunderstandings when people from different cultures attempt to work together.

Take space. For people in the United States, our ideas about communicating across space are so consistent that they can be charted like this:

COMMUNICATING ACROSS SPACE IN THE U.S.		
Distance	**Appropriate Voice**	**Appropriate Content**
very close (3–6 inches)	soft whisper	top secret
close (8–12 inches)	audible whisper	very confidential
near (12–20 inches)	indoors: soft voice; outdoors: full voice	confidential
neutral (20–36 inches)	soft voice, low volume	personal subject matter
neutral (4.5–5 feet)	full voice	information of nonpersonal matter
public distance (5.5–8 feet)	full voice with slight overloudness	public information for others to hear
across the room (8–20 feet)	loud voice	talking to a group
stretching the limits (20–24 feet indoors; up to 100 feet outdoors)	shouting	hailing distance; departures

Adapted from p. 179 of *The Silent Language.*

BRAIN TICKLERS
Set # 4

1. For each of the eight distance/voice/ content entries in the chart on page 20, describe a situation that matches well.
2. For each of the six key elements of communication that different cultures view differently (listed below), explain your own views on the element of communication (this may take some thinking if you haven't considered it before), tell any problems you've had in this area that could be because of cultural differences, and then describe how you might change your own behavior or respond differently to others now that you know that different cultures have different ideas about it.
a. punctuality
b. distance between people conversing
c. tone of voice
d. gestures
e. fun and humor
f. deeply held beliefs

(Answers are on pages 42–43.)

Genderlect

Did you ever think that talking to boys (if you're a girl) or girls (if you're a boy) was (a) nearly impossible or (b) doomed to failure? Linguistics professor Deborah Tannen (*You Just Don't Understand: Women and Men in Conversation*, Ballantine Books, N.Y., 1990) claims that cultural divisions go beyond those of region, ethnic group, and class, and actually include gender. Not only are there dialects, says Tannen, but there are also genderlects. Tannen suggests that only by taking a cross-cultural approach to speech between males and females can we understand the kinds of communication failures that occur. That is, if we think about men and women—even if they grew up on the same street, in the same town, with the same ethnic background—as coming from different cultures and approach breakdowns in communication between them as being culturally based, we are more likely, Tannen thinks, to be able to find and deal with the issues that are getting in the way of understanding.

One of the differences that Tannen sees between women's and men's cultures of communication is her observation that women generally use language for connection and intimacy, while men generally use language for status and independence. Generally, according to Tannen, women see a lack of conversation as a lack of connection or rapport. Men, on the other hand, generally use talking to get and keep attention (pp. 76–77).

Tannen also explains that different people have different ideas about overlapping words in conversations, and according to her data, conversations rarely occur without word overlap. Some people tolerate overlap with ease and see it as evidence of involvement and participation in the conversation. Others object to what they consider an offensive interruption.

BRAIN TICKLERS
Set # 5

1. What assumptions do you have about the roles of men and women that might be shaping your communication in ways you haven't considered previously?
2. Does your experience match Tannen's observations about men and women's use of language? Explain.
3. How do you feel about overlapping words? Has overlapping ever been a problem in your conversations? Explain.

[Answers are on page 43.]

Etiquette

When we think of etiquette, the "magic" words *please* and *thank you* may be the first thing that comes to mind—phrases we learned at a very young age to smooth social interactions with peers and adults alike. But it is possible to understand conversational etiquette in a much more complete and sophisticated way. We could start from the very basis of human relationships: **respect**, **truth**, and **trust**. Later, when we get to know a person, we are free to rescind our respect, conceal the truth, and withdraw our trust if our best judgment tells us we should do so. But without being incautious, we will have the best chance of building a strong connection or a lasting relationship if we plant truth, trust, and respect firmly at the foundation.

So in the spirit of these three guidelines, we will find that there is a time to speak and a time to listen—this means both reciprocity (we each give and we each take) and turn-taking (no one uses up all the time or attention). If we follow these guidelines, we will also usually make time for civilities—as fits our own and our conversation partner's gender, dialect, and culture, and the level of formality that fits the situation. **Civilities** are the polite acts and expressions that help us move in and out of social situations and iron things out when things are uncomfortable. Generally we greet a person when we first see them (*hello, good morning, what's up?, ¿qué tal?*), and speak words of parting (*goodbye, so long, later, au revoir*) when we leave. Usually we take care of what's most important first, which may mean personal items before "business" or vice versa, depending on the situation. We often continue threads of conversation that have been important between us in the past and introduce new items that we know or believe to be of interest. We apologize if we've done something that we feel uncomfortable about, or if we've caused discomfort for someone else. And we're considerate of the other person's time frame and agenda.

Cooperative conversation

Herbert Paul Grice, professor at Oxford and University of California, Berkeley, in an essay "Logic and Conversation" (*Studies in the Way of Words*, Harvard UP, 1989), proposed a **cooperative principle** for conversation that can help conversation participants create a mutually satisfying exchange. The cooperative principle states: "Make your conversational contribution such as is required, at the stage at which it occurs, by the accepted purpose or direction of the talk exchange in which you are engaged" (p. 26). This just means that our contributions to conversation should be guided by the conversational context. How do we do this? Grice proposes four categories of cooperation to guide people in being considerate conversationalists. In each category he suggests one or more maxims (pp. 26–27).

MAXIMS OF CONVERSATION	
Categories	**Maxims**
Quantity	1. Make your contribution as informative as is required (for the current purposes of your exchange). 2. Do not make your contribution more informative than is required.
Quality	Try to make your contribution one that is true. 1. Do not say what you believe to be false. 2. Do not say that for which you lack adequate evidence.

MAXIMS OF CONVERSATION, cont.	
Categories	**Maxims**
Relation [of material to conversation]	Be relevant.

Manner	Be perspicuous. [plainspoken]
	1. Avoid obscurity of expression.
	   [Use words your audience knows.]
	2. Avoid ambiguity. [Don't say things that
	   could be easily misunderstood.]
	3. Be brief (Avoid unnecessary prolixity*).
	4. Be orderly.

Prolixity means unnecessary length.

Philosopher A. P. Martinich suggested in an article ("Conversational Maxims and Some Philosophical Problems," *The Philosophy Quarterly*, Vol. 30, No. 120, pp. 215–228) that the maxim on relevance would benefit from two sub-maxims:

- Make your contribution one that moves the discourse toward its goal.
- Express yourself in terms that allow your hearer to tie your contribution into the conversational context.

When communicating with someone through an interpreter—whether your conversation partner is using a spoken language you are not fluent in or a signed language—remember to always look at the person with whom you are having the conversation, NOT at the interpreter, even though your eyes will naturally be drawn to the person who is speaking the language you recognize. This is an important etiquette rule for working with interpreters. It is appropriate to thank the interpreter at the conclusion of the conversation.

Just because the suggestions in this section are in language pertaining to conversation, doesn't mean that you can't apply them equally to other kinds of communication. Consider them for speeches, interviews, and letter writing, among other uses.

MODES OF COMMUNICATION

In 1983, in a book called *Frames of Mind,* Professor Howard Gardner of Harvard University introduced his theory of multiple intelligences. He proposed that, rather than a single kind of intelligence that people either possess or don't, there are actually seven kinds of intelligence:

- linguistic (verbal)
- musical
- logical-mathematical
- spatial
- bodily-kinesthetic
- interpersonal (understanding other people)
- intrapersonal (understanding one's own inner life)

With Gardner's work, more people began to understand that it isn't just a question of being "smart" or "not smart," and that school is not the only arena in which intelligence can play a role.

When speaking about communication, it is useful to employ a different set of capabilities that overlap with some of Gardner's:

the three **performance modes**—vocal, kinesthetic (movement), and emotional. Because we think about communication as being perceived through hearing and seeing, we look for a match between those senses and the ways in which people can communicate. There is an obvious match between hearing and the voice. But what we can *see* falls into several areas—we can see movement and action, but we can also see facial expressions, gestures, and other behaviors that signal emotion. The chart shows the relationship between our capabilities as communicators and Gardner's intelligences.

RELATING THE SEVEN INTELLIGENCES TO THE THREE PERFORMANCE MODES		
Name of performance mode	**Intelligence(s) used by speaker***	**Intelligence(s) used by listener***
vocal	linguistic	linguistic
kinesthetic	bodily-kinesthetic	bodily-kinesthetic
emotional	interpersonal and intrapersonal	interpersonal and intrapersonal

*Other intelligences may also be involved.

Though each of us may initially be more capable in one or another of the three performance modes, it is an excellent strategy to become as competent as possible in all three modes in order to best communicate with listeners/audiences with different intelligences. And the same applies for listeners, who use the performance modes as **response modes**. Suppose that you are an interpersonally intelligent person but are talking to a person whose strength is linguistic intelligence. Each of you, in turn, needs to perceive as best you can what the other is communicating in a mode that is not your strength.

BRAIN TICKLERS
Set # 6

1. Restate the cooperative principle and the maxims of conversation in your own words.
2. To identify your dominant mode, use these questions to help you think about your natural tendencies. Qualify your answers if necessary. Create a self-analysis.
   a. Do I learn best by seeing, by doing, or by hearing?
   b. Do I express myself most easily with words, by actions/gestures, or in music, drawing, or some other nonverbal artistic media?
   c. Among the arts, do I prefer to observe performances of music, presentations of dance or plays, or exhibits of paintings or other fine art?
   d. When faced with a dilemma or difficult decision, what problem-solving approaches and strategies do I use to evolve a plan?
   e. What do I find most distracting when I'm trying to concentrate: sounds, sights, or movements?
   f. What do I do when I'm bored?
   g. What memory strategies do I use?
   h. How do I act in new situations? Do I look around? touch things? listen to what's going on?
   i. How do I express myself when I feel strong emotions: with my voice? with my body? with facial expressions?
   j. How do I best understand how other people are feeling? Do I rely on what they say? what they do? how they look?

(Answers are on page 43.)

INTERNAL FEELING AND EXTERNAL COMMUNICATION

When we discussed incongruities and discrepancies between verbal and nonverbal communication (pages 14–15), we mentioned that people do not always convey their inner feelings, and that in some contexts it is entirely appropriate for people to be less than fully informative. Now, we need to speak more carefully about this matter of correspondence between our inner feelings and our communication to the world. Looked at from one perspective, there are three ways we can speak: in our own person; as an actor, purposefully taking on a personality that is not our own; or on behalf of another person or organization for a specific purpose or project. Each of these ways of speaking brings up certain issues about internal-external correspondence.

Speaking in your own voice

We have spoken about **dialect**—the language that distinguishes people from different regions, and **genderlect**—the language that distinguishes men and women. But did you know that there is also **idiolect**—the idiosyncratic or uniquely individual language that distinguishes one person from another? Nobody in the world—past, present, or future—ever has or ever will use language exactly the way you do.

Idiolect

In the last two decades of the twentieth century, much attention focused on the criminal known as the Unabomber. For seventeen years, Ted Kaczynski anonymously attacked university scientists and engineers with a barrage of mail bombs. The case was cracked and the terrorist identified when his sister-in-law recognized Ted's voice—in his writing. We're used to thinking about *voice* as meaning the sound of the spoken voice. What does *voice* in writing, also called **idiolect**, mean?

Don Foster, one of the leading experts in textual analysis—also called *literary forensics* when it's used to catch criminals—in his book *Author Unknown* (Henry Holt & Co., 2001), identifies elements of writing that make a person's writing unique and identifiable. Every one of these elements has a corresponding element in speech. This is not to say that people speak exactly as they write but that we leave our fingerprints—or more accurately, our "voiceprints" (or "signprints")—on our communications.

ELEMENTS OF AN IDIOLECT	
Element	**Description**
vocabulary	regionalisms, invented words, foreign words, characteristic interjections
thoughts	ideas and phrases used so often that their expression is ritualized
spelling	how accurately we write words
orthography	the look of our writing
mistakes	characteristic misspellings, faulty constructions, misuse of punctuation, etc.
grammar	pronoun agreement, sequence of verb tenses, avoidance of dangling participles, characteristic sentence constructions, etc.
sentence length	use of long, short, varied sentence length—related to sentence construction and grammatical choices

ELEMENTS OF AN IDIOLECT, cont.	
Element	**Description**
punctuation	characteristic use of punctuation, such as quotation marks, carets, cross-outs, dashes, ellipses, hyphens, commas, periods, semicolons, slashes, spaces, exclamation points, question marks, and interrobangs* (?!)
sources	use of quotations, ideas, and thought patterns (as well as misunderstandings and misapplications) from written sources, speeches, television, radio, movies, songs, teachers, etc.
tone	tendency to particular tones, such as sarcasm (see chart on pages 4–5)

*An interrobang is a combination of a question mark and an exclamation mark (called a "bang" by printers) used as the end mark for exclamatory rhetorical sentences.

BRAIN TICKLERS
Set # 7

Are you aware of any idiosyncracies—either habits of speech or choices—that make your language recognizable to others—anything that shouts *this is me!* every time you write or open your mouth? Ask a couple of friends to help you discover what makes your language unique.

[Answers are on page 43.]

Choices in reflecting the inner self

Of the three different speech approaches—speaking as ourselves, speaking in an acting role, and speaking as a representative—the first option, speaking in our own person, gives us the most freedom to match our external expression to our internal feelings. But that doesn't mean that we should always say everything we think or feel or use the language that first comes to mind to convey that content. Let's focus on this for a moment.

Some people defend what they may call "expressing themselves honestly." To them, this means saying whatever is on their minds in whatever language they find appealing, even though others may find their thoughts out of place in the conversation context and their language offensive or inappropriate.

It helps to make a distinction between self-expression, on the one hand, and communication, on the other. When you're expressing yourself, which is often best done in private, you don't need to be concerned with anyone else. Sometimes having a rant about something can make people feel better. But when you're communicating, there's an audience for your words, and taking both the situation and their standards into account along with your feelings is a fundamental part of the process. If you choose to ignore your audience's preferences and the conversation context, your communication may not be effective. This can happen even if your audience would completely agree with or sympathize with your content, but the language you have chosen to express it offends them or the time and place you have chosen to speak about it is inappropriate. See the section Communicating Negative Content, pages 34–39, for more on this topic.

Learning to balance honesty and authenticity with the control necessary to show respect for the external situation and others' desires and needs is a process of lifelong learning. When and how and how much of our interior selves to reveal is never a question we can answer once and for all. We have to continually find a balance between a healthy expression of emotions and over-sharing: sharing may be a relief for the person getting something off his or her chest, but at the same time, TMI can be a burden for the listener.

Speaking in character: The actor in everyone

Acting requires us to use our voices and bodies to convey thoughts and feelings that are not our own. When we take on an acting role, we agree to portray given material at a given time using our bodies and voices, regardless of our own internal feelings at that time. If you chose to act, it is virtually certain that at some point, and possibly often, acting may require you to be convincingly happy when you're actually scared, tired, or heart-broken, for example. This is different from the situation we discussed earlier when a person is concealing his or her feelings and being untruthful. When we are acting, we are—and others know we are—playing a role. Our performance should be judged by how well we communicate what we were trying to/directed to communicate—that is, by our acting skill.

Acting includes putting aside your internal feelings and taking on roles of people who do and say things you would never do and say, but that doesn't mean that you should be willing to do anything whatsoever on the basis that "it's just a role." It's best to study a role before you accept it to make sure it's a good fit, if you have the opportunity. And if you find some element of the role unsettling for any reason, speaking to the director about your concerns is a good approach. If that does not clear up the issue, get some advice from someone you trust.

Speaking on behalf of others

Suppose you and your siblings want to convince your parents to get a frog. Suppose you're elected student council president. Suppose you become a member of the board of the local parks and recreation department. Well, it could happen! And then you might end up representing the group in public.

When you speak on behalf of others, you often end up with a mix in terms of representing yourself and representing the group as a whole. You may agree absolutely with some of the things

you state and feel not so supportive of other things you find yourself saying because the majority supports them. It's like a combination of speaking for yourself and acting—and if it helps, you might try thinking about your role in this way. Some of the time, when your internal feelings match your communication, you can speak wholeheartedly in your own voice. At other times, when you have to say something that contradicts your personal stance, you may have to draw on memories of other times and project, not your own feelings at the moment, but the communication that you have agreed to give on behalf of the group—in other words, you need to act.

COMMUNICATING NEGATIVE CONTENT

Has anyone ever said to you,

> "If you don't have something nice to say, don't say it."

This expression urges us not to include negative content in our communications. And it's worth considering that not every thought that comes into our heads has to come out of our mouths. But is it always wrong to say something negative? Clearly not.

It is unfortunate, however, that while building a foundation of respect, truth, and trust and following the cooperative principle and maxims of conversation provide us with guidance in many situations, they don't offer a lot of assistance in knowing how best to communicate negative content. The fact is, expressing negative thoughts and feelings is one of the biggest communication challenges, so it's worth learning how to communicate negative content effectively.

While we're undertaking this, though, it's important to distinguish communicating negative content from communicating in a negative way: communicating negative content does not mean you're communicating negatively. We'll talk more about communicating negatively in discussing bullying, below, and in the section "Avoiding communication problems" in the next chapter.

Let's begin by characterizing types of negative content. Once we're clear about what types of negative content we're dealing with, we can consider how to communicate it most effectively.

1. Bad news. Whether you broke your arm and are going to have to disappoint the other members of your band because you can't play drums for six weeks or your dog died and you have to tell your little brother, sometimes you're going to be the one who has to share the bad news.

2. Bad feelings. Whether you're feeling gloomy or sick or sad or angry or frustrated, sometimes saying "I'm fine" just isn't true.

3. Negative evaluation. Sometimes you just don't like the same movie or song or car or shirt or hamburger your friends do.

4. Confession. All of us make mistakes and bad choices on occasion, and sooner or later it's usually appropriate to 'fess up.

5. Embarrassing fact. If someone forgot to close a zipper, has spaghetti sauce on his chin, or put on her sweater inside out, it might be awkward to tell him or her, but possibly better than just letting it go.

6. Confrontation. If someone did something inappropriate, wrong, or embarrassing that you feel needs to be addressed, having a discussion with the person is one option.

We can separate out bullying from other types of negative communication, because bullying just should not happen. Bullies use their strength or status to violate others through namecalling and insults, ostracism, intimidation and threats, spreading rumors, and/or causing physical harm to people or possessions. Verbal bullying can harm others in serious ways, damaging someone's self-esteem, ruining someone's reputation, and even driving people to harm themselves. The fact is, this list of ways that bullies communicate makes a great short-list of a) ways of communicating negatively and, therefore, b) communication techniques you should avoid.

Now that we've sorted out some of the different types of negative content, let's discuss how you might communicate negative content in various situations.

Negative content when the stakes are low

When thinking about sharing negative content, one thing to consider is the effect of your words. For example, at any kind of public event there's something we might call the Oooh-Aaah effect. Oooh-Aaah is what crowds of people say when they are watching fireworks together. The fact of being in a large group enjoying the same show contributes to everyone's level of pleasure. Ever tried watching the fireworks alone? It's just not the same thing.

So, say you're at a concert with friends. They're enjoying the opening act, but you're not—you think it's pretty poor, and you can't wait for it to finish and the main attraction to come on. You could say how you feel. But your friends are all in the Oooh-Aaah zone, so think about what the effect of your words would be. Simply stating your displeasure will not make you like the concert better, but it is likely to make the concert less enjoyable for your friends. This is a time when keeping quiet might be a reasonable option.

But what if one of your friends asks for your opinion? You still have a choice about how you answer. You could say, "This band stinks like a cesspool" and have a good shot at ruining your friend's mood or you could go with "Only x minutes left till the main act; I'm so excited!"—a truthful statement that focuses on what you find positive and doesn't squelch your friend's fun.

Negative content when personal feelings are involved

What about more personal issues, where what's on the line isn't just the mood, but somebody's feelings? In this type of case, it partly depends on your relationship and history with the person asking. For example, if you have a friend or family member who is colorblind and who checks with you to make sure that he or she hasn't chosen a really odd combination of colors, then that person is counting on you to be honest, even if your evaluation is negative.

Sometimes we're simply put on the spot when there isn't a history to go by and our honest response is negative. Then what? Here are some approaches:

- Some people advise the "little white lie" to cover social occasions in which saying the truth could result in hurt feelings.

- If you don't like or admire something you are asked about, you can choose to comment only on a facet of it that you can honestly praise.

- You can also say something equivocal, that is, something that has two meanings, one of which will seem like praise to the person hearing it. Exclamations like *wow* or *will you look at that* and adjectives like *interesting* can be taken as praise by your audience, even though you haven't actually stated any praise. But beware: this is a kind of trick, so while it can get you out of a social jam, you should be careful if you consider using it.

- Alternatively, you could honestly praise the person's choice/performance/etc. on another occasion to escape having to comment on this occasion.

- You could also try to get out of it by trying to show that your opinion isn't really worth much in the situation. Optionally, you can follow this up by asking for instruction on how to form an opinion about the kind of thing you're being asked about.

Which approach you choose may depend on your upbringing and your beliefs about lying. Here are examples for each approach:

SITUATION: You're babysitting for a seven-year-old who points to a piece of artwork on the fridge and asks,
QUESTION: Do you like it?

You're on the spot. You don't like it at all, but you're talking to a little kid, and you're in a position of responsibility. How might you answer?

Answers:

- **Telling a little white lie:** Oh, yes. (Private thought: It's awful.)
- **Praising a facet honestly:** I really like the colors you chose. (Private thought: But the rest is awful.)
- **Equivocating:** Wow! I've never seen anything like it! It's really something! (Private thought: It's awful.)
- **Praising something else:** You know that drawing of a tiger you made for me last week will always be my favorite. (Private thought: It's awful.)
- **Downplaying the value of your opinion:** It's not my favorite, but it's most important that you be happy with it, and I can see that you are. *or* You shouldn't ask me about things like this; I always say the wrong thing when people ask me about art. But since you know more about this picture than anyone, how about if you tell me how you went about making it?

You can adapt these suggestions to suit various situations.

Negative content when the stakes are high

Sometimes the situation is more tenuous than those we've been considering, often because the negative content you have to communicate is more important and there is a higher risk that the person you have to tell will not react well. Here are some examples of situations in which saying something negative may seem necessary but risky:

Situation 1:   You (accidentally) damaged property that belongs to someone else (you backed your car into someone's mailbox).

Situation 2: Something was entrusted to your care and something bad happened to it (while you were house-sitting, a canary died).

Situation 3: You can't fulfill a promise you made (you agreed to work on an English project that's due tomorrow at the same time that you have to go to the orthodontist).

Situation 4: You did something wrong that you need to come clean about (you looked at someone else's journal).

Situation 5: Someone did something bad to you, and you need to address it (someone broadcast a private e-mail you had sent).

Situation 6: A document or presentation that you were asked to check needs much more revision than the creator can possibly complete before the due date (your friend's job application letter, due tomorrow, is full of errors).

People spend a lot of time agonizing over important negative communications like these, particularly because the audience may be unprepared to accept the negative information and may react badly. You can help make your communication effective and control the outcome by thinking about the way you communicate the negative content and the context in which you choose to communicate it. Following are seven key choices over which you have some control and which can help you to communicate important negative content with the best possible results. You are more likely to have success in communicating important negative information if you:

1. focus on communication rather than self-expression, thinking about **the effect your communication choices will have** on your audience;
2. speak **in private**, where you won't be overheard;
3. speak at a place and in a moment that **allows sufficient time for your audience to process** the information;
4. **provide an introduction** that gives your audience a chance to prepare for what's coming, "cushioning the blow" if necessary;
5. communicate using a **considered style** (tone and diction);
6. address the issue in a **timely** way; and
7. if appropriate, **apologize and/or offer to assist** with the problem or situation.

BRAIN TICKLERS—THE ANSWERS

Set # 1, pages 8–9

Answers will vary. Possible response:

1. a.

Vocal Element	First Reading	Second Reading
	"as if scared"	"as if enthusiastic"
Language	same	same
Pitch	high, squeaky	lower, closer to normal
Volume	soft	loud
Tempo	fast	a little slower
Tone	fearful	enthusiastic
Stress	minimal	more
Timbre	not much air	full and hearty
Silence	no pauses	pauses for emphasis

   b. First reading: I paused between each sentence, increased the volume of my voice for each one, and used more stress in each one. Second reading: I also paused between each sentence, but I slowed the tempo and increased the volume for each one, making the tone richer and warmer.

   c. First reading: I increased the tempo and volume and stress as I went on. Second reading: I slowed the tempo, added pauses, lessened the volume and the level of stresses, and allowed my voice to weaken by using less breath.

   d. First reading: I decreased the volume from a yell, to a loud voice, to a conversational voice, with a pause between each, and also in the first sentence when I yelled, I elongated and stressed every syllable, but by the third sentence, I was speaking "normally." Second reading: I reversed my approach to the first reading (starting with a normal, conversational voice, and getting louder). I also changed my tone (I decided to be puzzled about why the person was running away), except for the last sentence: Instead of elongating, I did it like hammer strokes with a strong, sharp stress on every loud syllable, until the last syllable, which I held for a bit.

2. Answers will vary. **Possible response** (stressed word italicized):

Mom: I'm really quite sick of Peter's everlasting snakes.

Eric: Me, too. I don't like reptiles. I don't like their scales.

Mom: I don't much care for his toads either.

Eric: Me, too. I don't like amphibians.

Me: I'd like a furry pet.

Mom: Yes, furry and cuddly.

Eric: Me, too. I like mammals.

Mom: I think I'd like something that doesn't eat rodents or insects.

Me: We really ought to consider getting a pet *orangutan*.

3. Answers will vary. You should note the patterns, including repetition of words and sentence construction; and the meaning in terms of the history of our country, and why the Gettysburg Address is still important. It might be appropriate to read this at an occasion marking an historic day, an event honoring our country, a celebration of freedom, or a remembrance of veterans and their sacrifices.

Set # 2, page 10

Answers will vary. **Possible response:**

After I inhale, my respiratory muscles move the air through my vocal cords, creating sound waves. These sound waves are reinforced and amplified in my chest, throat, mouth, and nasal cavities, and then shaped by my movable and nonmovable articulators into recognizable speech sounds.

Set # 3, page 16

Answers will vary depending on which reporters are observed at which particular time(s). Answers should include comments on word choice, tone, tempo, pauses, interruptions with nonverbal markers like "uh" and "mmm," facial expression, posture, gestures, actions, clothing, and grooming.

Set # 4, page 21

1. **Possible responses:** very close—playing "telephone"; close—talking to a friend in the library reference room; near—planning a birthday present for my brother with my sister; neutral (a)—talking at work about something that happened at home; neutral (b)—talking at work about some work-related topic; public distance—asking a cashier for information; across the room—toasting someone on a special occasion; stretching the limits—calling family members in for dinner.

2. Answers will vary. Clearly express your own views and compare and contrast them with the views of those with whom you communicate. Then make reasonable suggestions.

Set # 5, page 22

Answers will vary. Clearly express your own views and compare and contrast them with the views of those with whom you communicate. Then make reasonable suggestions.

Set # 6, page 28

1. Answers will vary. **Possible response:** Choose what you say to help keep the conversation going. Don't say more or less than is necessary. Tell the truth and contribute information that is supported. Stay on topic. Choose your words in order to be clear and easily understood.

2. Answers will vary.

Set # 7, page 31

Answers will vary. The more careful the analysis, the more you will learn about your idiolect.

"Confer, Converse, and Otherwise Hobnob": Informal Talk with Others

HOW DOES COMMUNICATION HAPPEN?

Helen Adams Keller had a normal infancy in which she walked the day she turned one and learned a few words (including the word *water*). But when she was nineteen months old, she contracted scarlet fever, which nearly killed her and left her deaf and blind. Her communication with others became severely impaired. She not only lost the ability to speak and failed to learn any new words, but she also lost the understanding of the use of symbols to represent things. But then, in one amazing moment, this understanding came back. In *The Story of My Life*, she tells it in her own words:

> Some one was drawing water and my teacher placed my hand under the spout. As the cool stream gushed over one hand she spelled into the other the word water, first slowly, then rapidly. I stood still, my whole attention fixed upon the motions of her fingers. Suddenly I felt a misty consciousness as of something forgotten—a thrill of returning thought; and somehow the mystery of language was revealed to me. I knew then that "w-a-t-e-r" meant the wonderful cool something that was flowing over my hand. That living word awakened my soul, gave it light, hope, joy, set it free!

Audio and text versions of *The Story of My Life* are available online. (See the *Painless Speaking* website for current URLs.)

BRAIN TICKLERS
Set # 8

Write a brief essay telling the importance words and communication have had in your life.

(Answer is on page 85.)

A moment of understanding

Helen Keller's recollection shows us the smallest complete instance of communication—a moment of understanding in which two people comprehend the same word in the same way. This particular moment when Helen recognized the connection between the word *water* and the substance water fascinated Louisiana novelist and essayist Walker Percy. He used this one moment as the basis for a diagram capturing how communication works in general. Some of the words in the diagram may be unfamiliar. It may help if you substitute the words *Me* and *You* for Organisms 1 and 2; *Naming* for *Quasi Identity*; and *Mutual Understanding* for *Intersubjectivity*.

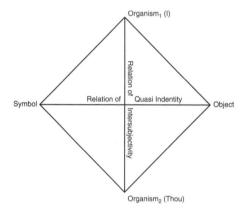

Diagram 1
The Intentional Relation of Identity. From Percy's essay "Semiotic and a Theory of Knowledge."

We might explain the diagram in words by saying, "When two people both identify a particular symbol (e.g., a word) with a particular object, then when one of them uses the symbol, they will mutually understand that the object is the intended reference."

To understand this concept more fully, let's go back to the particular example of Helen's moment of understanding, using this type of diagram. Diagram 2 shows before Helen understands and Diagram 3 shows after. The diagrams also show what Annie, the Communicator, and Helen, the intended Receiver of the communication are thinking. The ≈ in their thoughts shows that the symbol names the object.

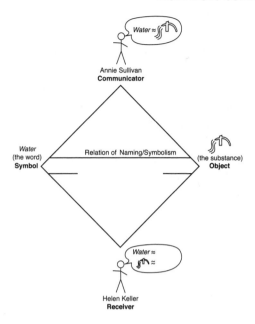

Diagram 2

Not Understanding. Helen can feel Annie fingerspelling and feel the water, but she doesn't connect them. So there is no communication and no understanding or "intersubjectivity."

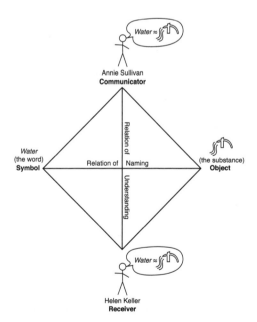

Diagram 3

Communication and Understanding Achieved. Annie and Helen share an understanding that *water* refers to the substance water.

Helen Keller didn't understand Annie Sullivan fingerspelling *water* because—due to her illness—she had lost the very idea of language as a way of naming objects. But that's not the only situation in which communication can fail. Think about a young child who is just learning to speak. There are many objects for which they might not know the name, and that situation could also be represented by Diagram 2.

But if we consider two people who don't use the same word for an object, then we have a different situation and we need a new diagram. Here's an example: A speaker of English names the substance water with the word *water*, but a speaker of Tok Pisin (a Creole language spoken in Papua New Guinea) names it *wara*. Diagram 4 shows this situation.

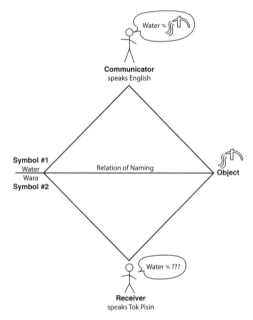

Diagram 4
Different Vocabulary. Each of these people has a symbol for the object: it's just not the same symbol.

You can see in this diagram that each person has a Relation of Naming for the object. But since neither one is shared by both the Communicator and the Receiver, communication fails.

There is one more situation of communication failure that we should consider. Sometimes, communication between people who share a symbol object relationship can be thwarted because of one of these problems:

- homophones (words that sound alike);
- small glitches in pronunciation;
- words that sound very similar spoken in a situation with background noise or distractions; or
- a mistake about context, like a Communicator mentioning a brother named Barry and the Receiver jumping to the conclusion that the reference was to a mutual friend named Perry.

An example of one of these types of communication failure is shown in Diagram 5.

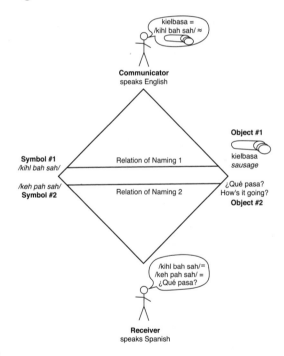

Diagram 5
Misunderstanding Due to Similarity of Words. The Receiver, acting in good faith, makes an incorrect identification of symbol and object because of confusing two words that sound very similar.

In the type of situation shown in Diagram 5, there are two different Relations of Naming that get confused with each other.

Preventing misunderstandings

Thinking about these diagrams and the situations they represent can sometimes help us to understand what has happened when communication fails, and in certain cases help us prevent such failures. The misunderstandings that are easiest to both prevent and fix are the type shown in Diagram 2. If you're speaking to someone who you know has limited vocabulary (like a young child or a nonnative speaker), you can try to choose words that will be easily understood. In addition, you can be alert for signs of confusion, which are often communicated in three ways: facial expression (frown, or look of confusion), body language, or words (the person may ask a question or use a nonverbal marker like *huh?*). If you suspect someone doesn't understand what you said, check in with them and see.

BRAIN TICKLERS
Set # 9

1. In various parts of the U.S., there are 12 different names for sandwiches served on crusty loaves: bomber, Cuban sandwich, grinder, hero, hoagie, Italian sandwich, muffuletta, poor boy (po' boy), sub, torpedo, wedge, and zep. Because there is no standard name, people could easily misunderstand each other, either not knowing what was being referenced if the word is unusual (zep or muffuletta) or—if the word has another meaning (hero, torpedo), thinking something quite different than a sandwich was the topic. Think of or research three other instances in which English speakers could misunderstand each other because they use different words to name the same object.

2. Create two conversations in which people mistake each other's meanings because of two words that sound nearly or exactly alike. Your examples may use people who speak the same dialect, different dialects, or different languages.

(Answers are on page 85.)

Limitations of the "Moment of Understanding" diagram

We've seen how useful the Percy diagram and adaptations of it can be in helping to understand successful and unsuccessful communication. Nevertheless, there are four important limitations to this visualization of the communication process.

First, communications are made with a purpose—a desired outcome that our single-word examples don't touch on. Second, communications are usually longer and more complex than our single-word examples and have structures and styles that we need to consider. Third, in a single moment, with a single word, we can view one person as being the Communicator and the other as being the Receiver of the Communication, but in reality both people in a two-person conversation usually take on both roles. And fourth, communication usually takes place over time, not in a single moment, so we need to consider individual communications as part of a chain that may take place over days, weeks, or longer and involve more than two people. These four points show us that we need to develop a more sophisticated understanding to match the complexity of real-life communication.

Finding a unit of communication

If a single word is too small a unit of language to focus on in order to capture the complexity of language interactions, what should we look at as a unit of communication? It might seem that the sentence is worth considering, especially since you have probably heard that "a sentence is a complete thought," and that seems to give it promise as a communication building block. But there are problems with the choice of a sentence. Here's why.

Sentences are defined as being "complete thoughts" in an effort to distinguish them from fragments and run-ons. Fragments are said to be incomplete because they are lacking a subject, a predicate, or both, and so, the reasoning goes, cannot be complete thoughts. Run-ons are said to include multiple thoughts because they have two or more independent clauses that are not properly joined. But there's some confusion here: The idea of a complete grammatical construction is being confused with a complete thought, even though the completeness of a thought logically has nothing to do with grammar, but with whether a concept has been fully enunciated.

In fact, there's no reason why a complete grammatical construction—a properly formed sentence—cannot be either more or less than a complete thought. Look at this communication, which (according to the rules of grammar) is a fragment, and therefore not a complete thought:

Ouch!

What's incomplete about it? Good question! There is no subject, but we know who the subject is: the person who yelled. There's no verb, but we know that the verb is *hurt*. We could create a complete sentence:

Ouch, I hurt myself!

But why should we? *Ouch!* does a perfectly fine job of communicating everything we need to know. We could easily argue that *Ouch, I hurt myself* is more than a complete thought—it avoids the fragment, but it's redundant.

Now let's examine a longer piece of writing, the 267-word Gettysburg Address (page 253). The speech has ten grammatically complete sentences, but this does not mean that it has ten separate, conceptually complete thoughts. In fact, we can prove that it doesn't. If we look at just one of the sentences—

It is altogether fitting and proper that we should do this.

—we find that the final word, *this*, is a demonstrative pronoun that points to an antecedent outside of the sentence. So how does it make sense to talk about this sentence as a complete thought when crucial material for understanding it is elsewhere in the address? In fact, it seems most reasonable to treat the address as a whole *and* to analyze it not by itself but as a response to what came before.

Hopefully it is now clear that the famous rule about sentences being complete thoughts doesn't work, and the fact that something either less or more than a sentence can be needed for a complete thought means we need to go with some other entity as our unit of communication. I propose the "utterance," a unit of communication put forward by Russian linguist Mikhail Bakhtin and explained in his essay "The Problem of Speech Genres" (in *Speech Genres and Other Late Essays*, University of Texas Press, 1986, pp. 60–102).

Defining an utterance

Let's begin by introducing some vocabulary so that our discussion of the utterance can proceed without interruptions. First, let's clarify that—like a word or sentence—an utterance can be spoken, written, signed, etc. Since the term *communicator* is awkward and since Bakhtin uses *speaker* to name the person who's communicating, we will, too, with the understanding that the speaker may be speaking, writing, signing, etc. And we will use *addressee*, as Bakhtin does, for the audience for whom the communication is meant, rather than *listener*, because *listener* is so strongly associated with passive taking-in. We'll call the form of the utterance (for example, a poem, a farewell address, or a how-to explanation) a *speech genre*, as Bakhtin does, even though it may be written or signed.

Definition of an utterance. An utterance is one link in a chain of communication and includes everything a speaker wants to say to an addressee on a given subject or theme in the current context in order to achieve some desired response. The utterance is made in a particular speech genre that the speaker chooses to fit the content, the addressee, the desired response, and the context. The utterance has boundaries at its beginning and end, sometimes in very obvious wording (such as "Once upon a time" and "the end" in fairy tales), but sometimes just signaled by the fact that the speaker stops and someone else speaks or there is silence.

To summarize, an utterance:

- is a link in a chain of communication;
- is the speaker's complete communication on the topic, adapted to the context, and with clear boundaries at the beginning and end; and
- is created to elicit a response from the addressee.

Let's explore each of these points.

A link in the chain

It stands to reason that this speaker we are talking about has been an addressee in the past and will be again in the future. In fact, any particular utterance is best conceived as a link in a long chain of communications, or—even better—a web of communications that includes all the communications that speaker and addressee have each participated in throughout their lives. Why a web? Because Bakhtin—like Don Foster, who analyzed idiolects—

believes that a key role is played by the influences of past utterances each speaker has made and had addressed to him or her.

In *Author Unknown*, Foster enunciates this view (using the word *texts* to refer to any collection of words, whether in print or performed) when he says (p. 13),

> . . . the mind of the writer . . . cannot be understood without first inquiring after the texts, including television, film, and even music CDs, by which that mind has been conditioned. You are what you read. When you write, your reading leaves its imprint on the page.

What Foster says of the mind of the writer is, Bakhtin would say, equally true of the mind of the speaker. And he would also emphasize the role of past conversations.

Finalization

The idea that an utterance is everything the speaker has to say at the particular time and in the particular circumstances allows for a quality that Bakhtin calls **finalization.** *Finalization* has three parts, and when they're fulfilled the utterance has been presented in a way that sets the stage for a response: it is presented in a finalized state, it is adapted to fit the context and addressee, and it fulfills any requirements of the speech genre that is used.

The first part of finalization is presenting the utterance in **final form.** For casual utterances, like conversation, the final form may be the only form, but for utterances in genres that include preparation, it's different. For example, you don't expect your teacher to give you a final grade on your research report when you hand in an outline or a first draft. At those stages, you are still developing "everything you have to say at the particular time and in the particular circumstances" concerning your topic. It is only on the due date, when you hand in your final draft, that your utterance is finalized and your teacher gives you a final grade. Similarly, for a play, rehearsals are a time during which the utterance is still being developed: it's not ready for response until it's performed. Even in a conversation, which doesn't usually have rehearsals, people may realize that they misspoke, saying something that didn't represent their true thoughts, and seek to clarify because they're not satisfied that their earlier utterance was finalized. If someone corrects him- or herself, then the correction becomes the finalized version.

Sphere is the word Bakhtin uses to denote different contexts with different addressees, and utterances should fit the sphere in which they're presented. If someone were running around talking to people about a lost rabbit, the topic would be consistent in all the conversations. But we would expect the topic to be discussed differently with a little child, a best friend, a parent, and the animal control supervisor for the area. This adaptation to context and audience is necessary in order to set the stage for response. For example, what if the rabbit owner said to a three-year-old neighbor,

If you should chance to perceive a member of the Leporidae family—specifically, a female Valenciano giant with the appellation Timora— I would be most gratified if you would notify the appropriate authorities posthaste.

In this case, the utterance isn't finalized because the speaker hasn't made good communication choices: no toddler could understand what the speaker said, and without understanding, there's no possibility of response. It's also possible for an utterance to be in final form and appropriate to the sphere but fail to gain a response if the addressee fails to pay attention or it's too noisy to hear.

Finally, we need to consider **required elements**. If the speaker has chosen to make the utterance in a speech genre that has required parts (like a business letter, which needs a date, an inside address, a salutation, etc.), the utterance is not finalized—even if it is presented in a final form (e.g., typed up, placed in an envelope, stamped, and mailed)—if parts are missing.

We can now summarize the differences between a sentence and an utterance. A sentence is a unit of language, while an utterance is a unit of communication. A sentence is complete when its grammatical form is properly realized, while an utterance is complete when it is finalized. A sentence may be an utterance, but an utterance may be more or less than a sentence.

One thing to note: If you allowed me to interrupt you for clarification, the speaker would have changed, but your utterance would not be complete because finalization would not have occurred. The interruption would be like a time-out, and when we had cleared up whatever point I raised, you'd have a chance to finish your utterance.

Response to an utterance

Now that we've delved into what an utterance is, let's turn to the role of the addressee. Bakhtin proposes the addressee as an active respondent, sooner or later speaking or acting in a way that takes the utterance he or she heard or read into account. The type of response depends on several factors, including the content of the utterance, the addressee's reaction to the utterance, including the speaker's tone and presentation, and the importance of what was communicated. A range of responses is to be expected for three reasons:

- because utterances range from trivial (I ate three grapes.) to extremely important (Call 911!);
- because speakers have different effects in mind when they create utterances; and
- because some utterances are more effective than others.

SOME WAYS TO RESPOND TO AN UTTERANCE

affirm it	discuss it	reinterpret it
analyze it	evaluate it	relate it to other things
apply it	examine it	rely on it
appraise it	execute it	reorganize it
arrange it	explain it	select it
assess it	integrate it	solve it
believe it	investigate it	summarize it
build it	laugh	supplement it
build on it	practice it	support it
categorize it	presuppose it	teach it
consider it	produce it	translate it
criticize it	prove it	use it
cry	quote it	verify it
demonstrate it	rank it	weigh it
develop it		

BRAIN TICKLERS
Set # 10

For each sentence or fragment, create a conversational context in which it can stand as an utterance.

1. Ah!   5. Ugh!   9. Yup.

2. Ouch!   6. That's true.   10. Great!

3. Take care.   7. Dunno.

4. Huh!   8. Thank you.

(Answers are on pages 86–87.)

With all the different types of possible responses, how does a speaker attempt to evoke a particular type of response? There are many different ways a speaker can signal an addressee:

- choice of context for the utterance, e.g., public vs. private;
- speech genre chosen, e.g., business letter vs. personal letter;
- diction and style, e.g., formal language vs. informal language;
- content, e.g., specific requests for response, arguments for a particular position, instructions for doing something, etc.;
- sentence type.

It might be hard to imagine how sentence type could help convey the type of response desired, so here's an example. It's possible to frame a question in several different ways: a statement with a tag, a yes-or-no question, and an open-ended question. Each type of question encourages a different type of response. The statement with a tag encourages agreement. The yes-or-no question encourages a simple one-word response. And the open-ended question invites a fuller discussion.

A question that's too broad, on the other hand (What do you think about religion?), may leave an addressee tongue-tied because there's not enough context about where the conversation is heading.

BRAIN TICKLERS
Set # 11

1. Identify how you have used five different responses to an utterance at one time or another in your life.
2. Explain in as much detail as you can how you once crafted an utterance in order to try to evoke one type of response in particular.

(Answers are on page 87.)

THE ART OF CONVERSATION

Speech genres include weather reports, essays, songs, gossip, textbooks, and advertisements. We'll talk about them more beginning on page 94, but for the rest of this chapter we're going to focus on the wonderful, free-flowing speech genre of conversation, continuing the discussion we began in Chapter 1.

Bakhtin's ideas about utterances can help us to be good conversationalists because he gives us solid criteria for evaluating when someone is done speaking and for helping others understand when we have finalized our utterances. To this foundation, we can add some of his ideas about how to treat our addressees respectfully. He says, "When speaking I always take into account . . . whether [my addressee] is familiar with the situation, whether he has special knowledge of the given cultural area of communication, his views and convictions, his prejudices (from my viewpoint), his sympathies and antipathies—because all this will determine his active responsive understanding of my utterance" (pp. 95–96). By considering his addressee carefully, Bakhtin hopes to prepare an utterance that is suited for the addressee's needs, to make the communication as smooth as possible. He draws on his **prior knowledge** of his addressee to inform his decisions.

Looking from the same perspective

Another way in which we can be good conversationalists is to try to understand the perspective of our addressee. There are several ways in which we can do this, both figuratively and literally: by being aware of presuppositions, point of view, and levels of engagement.

Presuppositions

A **presupposition** is an assumption that must be true in order for an utterance to have validity. There are many reasons that a statement could be invalidated by a false assumption. Sometimes presuppositions are not stated in an obvious way. Here are some examples:

The question, Who is the present king of the United States? makes no sense because it has been a long time since, at great cost, we removed royalty as rulers in our country.

The question, Who turned off the lights? assumes that the lights were on recently.

The question, Have you bought another iguana? makes no sense unless the addressee has already purchased at least one iguana.

The statement, Joan no longer grows musk melons, rests on the assumption that once upon a time she did.

When you converse, be aware of assumptions that may be hidden in your utterances.

It all depends on your point of view: Deixis

If I say "my mom" and you say "my mom," we use exactly the same words, but we're talking about two different mothers.

Deixis (dike-sihs) refers to the pointing function of words, the meaning of which is affected by context. When I say *my* it means something different than when you say *my*. When **deictic** words are used, you need to know **who's** speaking, **who's** listening, or **both**, to be able to know what the words mean. Besides first- and second-person pronouns (*I, me, my, mine, you, your, yours, we, ours, us*), demonstrative pronouns (*this* and *that*) are also deictic. For **deixis** words referring to place, the meaning depends on **where** the speaker is (for example, *here, there, these, those, yonder, front, back, right, left*), and for **deixis** words referring to time (for example, *now, later, then, last week, next spring, tomorrow*), meaning depends on **when** they were spoken. By using these words thoughtfully, you can in-sure that your addressee knows what you mean.

Levels of engagement

Another important aspect of good con-versation is that all participants be in-volved to more or less the same depth. Finding the same depth can require careful attention because the nature of human interaction is

that we only see bits of each other's lives. We go away from each other, and when we come back into contact, we often have little idea about what has happened to the other person in the meantime. And we usually begin our conversations with what Don Miller, Senior Associate in political science at Melbourne University, calls **verbal readymades**—phrases that have been used and reused so much that they are habitual, that we hardly pay attention to them and barely expect an answer (Whassup, Hey, Hi, etc.). But here's the thing—although sometimes the answer may also be a verbal readymade, a toss-off, at OTHER TIMES, the answer may carry a cue that the speaker wants or needs to get off the readymade track and have a *real* conversation. This can happen for all kinds of reasons; for example, because something really important or interesting or crucial or wonderful or devastating happened in his or her life. Cues to look for include a slower tempo, longer sentences, content that alerts you that something's up, unusual pauses, or a direct request for a conversation.

Orality vs. literacy

Speaking is natural; writing isn't. Of the maybe tens of thousands of languages spoken in all of history, researcher Munro E. Edmondson claims that only about 106 have actually been written sufficiently to attain a body of work that could be called a literature. But because we're so used to writing, we may not have ever thought about the different demands of communicating orally as opposed to communicating in writing.

For helpful tips, we can turn to Walter J. Ong, whose book *Orality and Literacy: The Technologizing of the Word* (Routledge, 1988) contains a fine analysis of the strategies that work in situations in which nothing is written down.

Ong points out that when your addressee walks away from you, s/he will only know what s/he can recall from what you've said. This obvious fact, when considered carefully, suggests some concrete steps that can help your addressees retain more material—or at least the crucial bits you want them to remember.

HOW TO HELP LISTENERS REMEMBER
WHAT YOU SAID

Strategy	How to Carry It Out
Speak in patterns.	You can create patterns on the level of thoughts, words, or sentence constructions.
Incorporate mnemonics.	A **mnemonic** is an invention to aid memory. If you ask your sister to buy you shoelaces, a piece of orange poster board, and adhesive bandages, you could point out that the initials of the three items spell *sob* and tell her you will cry if she forgets to buy them for you.
Use repetitions or antitheses.	Pay attention to anything in your thoughts that has duplication, repetition, similarity, or opposition—and exploit it.
Use formulas.	Usually we want to avoid them, but clichés work for certain uses, and memory assistance is one.
Focus on the concrete rather than the abstract.	Concrete examples are easier to think about in the first place; therefore, they are easier to retain.
Encourage participation.	The listener who has been drawn into interaction is more likely to recall material.
Avoid complex analyses and many levels of subordination.	Any material that requires the listener to hold a great deal of preceding information and organize it within his or her mind makes recollection difficult. Such topics are more easily presented with graphic aids and written handouts.
Target your audience's level of understanding.	Although it's easy to look up a word, or even a handful of words, when you're reading in a quiet place, it's harder to grasp the flow of spoken communication if you have to keep interrupting to ask what words mean. Be a thoughtful speaker and try to be considerate of your audience's capabilities.

Understanding the communication circle

Michael Shurtleff, Broadway casting director, said it so well in his book *Audition* (Bantam Doubleday Dell, 1978, pp. 87–88):

"Communication is a circle, not a one-way street. You hear people say in life, 'But I told him!' as if telling *at* someone were sufficient. If he hasn't received what you've told him, there is no communication. It takes *two* to communicate: the sender and the receiver. The receiver has to acknowledge the message by sending a reply back to the sender, thus completing the circle before a communication has taken place. This imposes a constant obligation on the part of the sender to (1) make sure his message is clear and (2) check that the receiver has received it. And an obligation on the part of the receiver to (1) make sure he's heard the message and is able to *duplicate* it and (2) let the sender know he's received the message. ... Communication's not easy."

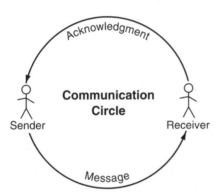

If all those involved in speech communication take responsibility for the communication working well, the burden doesn't fall on any one person—which it shouldn't. It's easiest to keep an eye on the communication circle in face-to-face conversation between only two people. But while you're considering communication as a circle, don't forget the link-in-the-chain concept of communication, which is also important.

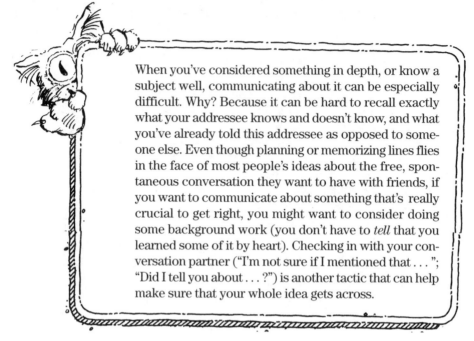

When you've considered something in depth, or know a subject well, communicating about it can be especially difficult. Why? Because it can be hard to recall exactly what your addressee knows and doesn't know, and what you've already told this addressee as opposed to someone else. Even though planning or memorizing lines flies in the face of most people's ideas about the free, spontaneous conversation they want to have with friends, if you want to communicate about something that's really crucial to get right, you might want to consider doing some background work (you don't have to *tell* that you learned some of it by heart). Checking in with your conversation partner ("I'm not sure if I mentioned that . . ."; "Did I tell you about . . . ?") is another tactic that can help make sure that your whole idea gets across.

Avoiding communication problems

Speech that comes across as offensive is not always meant to offend. How can this happen? There are several ways.

A person who is upset may experience "emotional spillover" and speak in an unpleasant or hostile tone to someone who has nothing to do with whatever the problem is. This can happen when people are very scared, rattled, or angry.

A person who is preoccupied or has certain types of developmental disorder that make it difficult to read social cues might speak too loudly or enter a conversation into which he or she hasn't been invited and isn't welcomed.

When a lot of secrets are being kept and some people are party to some but not to others, remembering who knows what can become very complex, and sooner or later somebody may make a mistake and say the wrong thing to the wrong person.

Keeping these possibilities in mind can help you to avoid either overreacting or misinterpreting speech situations that seem, at first glance, to be negative.

There are also ways of talking that have a tendency to destroy communication and break the circle. Dr. Thomas Gordon identified twelve of them:

TWELVE COMMUNICATION SPOILERS	
Spoiler	**Explanation**
criticizing	judging the person, the person's actions, or the person's attitudes
name-calling	using put-downs or stereotypes
diagnosing	analyzing in psychological terms, which most of us are not qualified to do
praising evaluatively	using praise as a stereotype, or in place of commenting on concrete accomplishments, artistic choices, and so on
ordering	commanding or demanding that the other person do as you wish
threatening	using the warning of negative consequences to try to force action
moralizing	giving advice in a condescending way by telling what should be done
excessive or inappropriate questioning	failing to respect another person's boundaries
advising	giving someone a solution, perhaps instead of allowing them to find their own answers
diverting	diminishing or dismissing the other's important issues
logical argument	responding with reasons that ignore the emotional content of the issues
reassuring	trying to stop negative emotions, whether or not they are justified

Since these responses aren't marked on people's sentences like labels on items in the grocery store, they can be hard to identify. What's more, people's reactions can be very individual. And with some response types—like praise, advice, and logic—there can be a fine line between what's appropriate and what's harmful. The best way to begin to learn about these spoilers is to pay attention to your own reactions when you feel others are being spoilers and to listen carefully if others react negatively to comments you make. And, since sometime or other each of us is likely to be hurt and, unfortunately, to cause pain or concern to another, it's important to be able to speak openly and carefully about feelings.

Talking about feelings

We can help deal appropriately with difficult subjects rather than spoil communications with negative responses if we can reach some level of comfort in talking about our own and others' feelings. For most of us, this is the work of a lifetime. One helpful tool is to have available words that name the subtle differences in the emotions that people feel. Then when you need to describe your inner state, at least you'll have a name for it.

AFRAID   CHEERFUL   CONCERNED   EMBARRASSED

MELANCHOLY   SUSPICIOUS   OUTRAGED   SURPRISED

HOW DO I FEEL?

absorbed	grief-stricken	relaxed
affectionate	guilty	relieved
afraid	happy	rested
aggravated	horrible	sad
angry	hurt	satisfied
betrayed	hysterical	scared
burdened	ignored	serene
cheated	imposed upon	shocked
cheerful	intimidated	spacey
compassionate	irritated	spiteful
concerned	itchy	stressed
connected	jealous	stunned
content	joyful	stupid
crushed	jumpy	surprised
defeated	lonely	sympathetic
despairing	loving	tense
disgusted	melancholy	thwarted
distraught	miserable	tired
dreadful	nervous	trapped
eager	numb	troubled
embarrassed	outraged	useless
exasperated	passionate	violated
excited	peaceful	vulnerable
fearful	persecuted	weepy
flustered	pressured	wonderful
foolish	proud	worried
frantic	rejected	

Types of conversation

We discussed conversations in Chapter 1, but let's review briefly. A **conversation** is an exchange of thoughts and feelings, often— but not always—in real time or something very close to it. When feelings are not included and the exchange is structured, as it often is in the workplace, the exchange is usually characterized as a conference or a meeting, rather than a conversation. A conversation is chiefly characterized by its back-and-forth nature, unlike certain speech genres in which a single person directs a message to one or more addressees (speeches, novels, lectures, etc.). Originally, all conversations were face-to-face, but today a variety of technologies allow people to interact across time and space. With so many different possibilities, perhaps the clearest way to define a conversation is "any exchange of communications that the participants treat like a conversation."

There are many ways to type conversations, some of which include:

- medium or media used;
- synchronous vs. asynchronous;
- formal vs. informal;
- spontaneous vs. planned;
- text only vs. voice only vs. voice and seeing the other person vs. text and file exchange, etc.;
- recorded vs. unrecorded;
- with others already known to you vs. with new acquaintances;
- at home vs. at work vs. at school.

Conversations can be simple or very demanding. Sometimes a friend comes over, and you easily plunge into a familiar discussion of your families, other friends, favorite TV shows, or plans you have for the weekend. It seems effortless, and you probably don't consider that you've "prepared" for the conversation, though in fact, all the knowledge you've gained about your friend for however many years you've been friends is coming into play as you talk. But talking to someone can also feel awkward if you don't know what to say next and there are long pauses or you have the feeling that the two of you are not understanding each other. So let's talk about conversation problems and how to fix or—better yet—avoid them.

How to have good face-to-face conversations

There are a few reasons that conversations run into problems. Just getting the conversation started can be difficult, particularly if the participants don't know each other well or at all, if there's a language barrier, or if there's some awkward feelings because of previous history. Issues that can arise at any point in a conversation include differing ideas about etiquette and failures in mutual understanding. Let's start at the beginning with getting a conversation going.

Getting to know you

Conversations get started in many different ways. Here are some:

- two people are introduced by a third;
- the leader of a group requires you to introduce yourself;
- one person recognizes another, although they've never met (Hey, are you Jen's kid brother? You look like her!);
- two people end up in the same place (e.g., at a bus stop);
- two people are independently pursuing the same activity;
- one person is interested in what the other is doing.

The first three cases are the only ones in which people are likely to do introductions "the old-fashioned way," giving their name, telling something about themselves, their relationship to the introducer, or why they're there, and providing some general history. For example, Sam introduces Frederic and Teresa.

Sam: Teresa, I'd like you to meet my new friend, Frederic Tulloch. Frederick, this is my neighbor, Teresa Lomedico.
Frederic: Nice to meet you, Teresa. I go by Fred, and I met Sam at baseball camp last summer.
Teresa: Pleased to meet you, Fred. You can call me Terry. Sam and I have lived on the same block since kindergarten.

Obviously, if we never spoke to strangers, we'd never meet anyone new, but it's wise to be cautious about giving out your name and other private information. Terry and Fred trust Sam, so they're happy to get on a nickname basis right off.

In the other situations, where you're starting from scratch, you might begin the conversation with opening lines that either refer to something that both of you are paying attention to or something you have in common. This could come from the place you're both in, the activity one or both of you are engaged in, general information, or news that's likely to be particularly interesting.

CONVERSATION OPENERS	
Type	**Examples**
Question arising from the situation	• That's a beautiful dog. Is it a Welsh corgi? • Have you seen the Essex bus? • Is that book as good as reviewers say?
Comment about the situation	• These lockers are too small! • I suggest you pass on the Salisbury steak . . . • What a lovely sunset!
Comment about generally interesting news or weather	• The new bicycle lane is due to open tomorrow. • There's supposed to be a cool meteor shower tonight. • It's supposed to be over 100°F tomorrow.
Newly acquired information that the other person would probably want to know	• Did you hear that French class is cancelled? • Did you know that Ms. Murphy is related to a former president?

After the opener

If the other person responds with something more than a grunt or a single syllable, his or her comment often provides material for your next response. Using any provided information to carry the conversation further is a good strategy when being introduced, too. For example, after Sam introduced Terry and Fred, Terry might ask Fred what position he plays, while Fred might ask Terry what Sam was like in kindergarten.

BRAIN TICKLERS
Set # 12

For each situation, give a greeting, introduction if appropriate, and a reason for getting to know the person, just as you might in actual conversation. Be sure to think about your audience and purpose and use wording that fits the situation.

1. It's your first day of physics class and you spot someone who you know is a really good student in math. You want to have a conversation that will end up with him or her being your lab partner.

Did you see the latest *Scientific American?*

2. You're asking the manager of a restaurant for a gift certificate for a fund-raising raffle.
3. You need to interview a politician for a news article for the local paper, so you're phoning your state's governor.
4. You see an adult walking down your street, looking lost.
5. You just saw someone do something illegal, and you're calling the police.
6. You're offering to volunteer at the local food kitchen on Saturday afternoons.

(Answers are on page 87.)

If, on the other hand, the person who you're trying to start a conversation with is unresponsive or walks away, it's best to let it go. Force is not a part of good communication.

If you are, or might be, romantically interested in a person and want to start a conversation with him or her, it's often best to use the same strategies you'd use with anyone else you want to get to know. Acting romantic when you're really not interested—the definition of *flirting*—is not honest, and may even be cruel if the other person doesn't take the situation as lightheartedly as you do.

BRAIN TICKLERS
Set # 13

Think of a scenario in which you might use each of these conversation openers and complete each sentence.

1. Could you show me how to ____?
2. They're predicting ____ this weekend, and ____.
3. I think the new ____ is really ____!
4. Do you want to go ____?
5. Do you remember when ____?
6. Did you ever ____?
7. Did you hear about ____?

(Answers are on page 88.)

After the introductions

Once the introductions are out of the way, conversation can go, well, just about anywhere. Conversation is the speech genre that includes the most other genres within it. Flexible and spontaneous, long or short, deeply intimate, casual, or businesslike, it sometimes starts with a greeting and a question about a person's well being and ends with a farewell, but in between—the sky's the limit. Stories, gossip, reviews, reports, complaints, jokes . . . just about anything goes. We're so used to moving easily from one speech genre to another within face-to-face conversation, that we may not even give too much thought to just how versatile a form it is.

Etiquette in face-to-face conversation

Occasionally it is necessary to interrupt a conversation, such as when someone else joins in. If the person has not yet met your original conversation partner, it's up to you to perform an introduction: A, I'd like you to meet B. B, this is my friend, A. Given an additional person, you will probably need to save private topics for later. If your private discussion can't wait, you can excuse yourself to the newly arrived party, saying that the matter you're discussing is urgent and that you will talk with him or her later.

If a conversation has to be cut short, it can be continued later—either in person or electronically.

Phone conversations and their etiquette

There are some obvious differences between phone conversation and face-to-face conversation:

- no cues from facial expression and body language
- the possibility of less privacy and the risk of disturbing others with the sound of the phone ringing or your voice as you're speaking
- a need to be considerate of others' need for the phone (and if the phone line has multiple uses, their need for the other devices that share it, like a computer or a fax machine)

With the spread of Caller ID services, unless you get a "private caller" message or an ID with a number and no name, you probably know who's calling before you even answer the phone. And with so many people having their own cell phones rather than sharing a landline, many callers know exactly who's going to pick up. This has caused a change in standard civilities for telephone use, which used to go something like this:

> **Receiver:** Hello?
> **Caller:** Hi. (This is Brad.) May I please speak to Toni?
> **Receiver:** Just a minute. (tells Toni: "Brad's on the phone.")
> **Toni:** Hi, Brad!

Today, this type of exchange is not needed in many cases. But for those times when you may be using a landline or calling a home that has one, it's useful to know the routine.

When you've reached the person you're calling, or he or she has reached you, conversations proceed pretty much as face-to-face conversations do, but without the visual cues. For this reason, you need to listen carefully to pick up vocal cues that signal emotions, the finalization of an utterance, and attitude—some of the things that are often communicated through facial expression and body language in face-to-face conversation.

The factors that have led to changes in phone etiquette have also led to changes in phone messages. Most phone messages are now left as voicemail on the dedicated phone of the individual or replaced with a text message. If you do end up taking a message for someone else, make sure you get the essential information: the caller's name, phone number, content of the message, and when the caller can be reached. Make sure the person receives the message as soon as possible.

E-mail and postal letter conversations and their etiquette

Postal mail and e-mail are both versatile and may range from formal to informal. For highly serious and sensitive communications, postal mail is sometimes preferred, but with the rise in acceptance of digital signatures, e-mail is not far behind. The etiquette of both forms varies with the purpose and content, and the best advice, when in doubt, is to follow the usage of the person who e-mailed you.

People use various methods to keep the sense of conversation in letters and e-mails, but quoting is the most common. Two methods are frequently used in e-mails. One is leaving the other person's e-mail intact below and responding above or vice versa. The second, which looks more like a conversation, interjects responses in between the sender's paragraphs (these show as a different color in most e-mail applications). In letters, the writer may be more likely to paraphrase, saying something like, "You mentioned calzone, and I have to say, it is one of my top five favorite meals."

People check their e-mail more or less often, and postal letters may take several days to a week or more to arrive, so only use these methods when time allows. When multiple people are involved in an e-mail conversation, "Reply All" can be used to send a response to everyone. To be selective about who receives your response, hit "Reply" instead, and add names as desired.

Instant messaging and its etiquette

Instant messages, or IMs, are part of a password-protected system of digital communication that is useful for intermittent or quick exchanges. Free to use and having no character limit, IMs are a useful alternative to text messaging or phone calls when all conversation participants are near their computers at the same time and allow more rapid exchanges than e-mail.

Although there's no character limit, the size of the text entry box and the awareness that the other person is waiting usually prompt IMers to write short answers, or divide answers up into small sections or paragraphs. For these reasons, it's not the best medium for complex, well-developed ideas. Especially when people are using small segments, it's important to pay attention to know when finalization has occurred. When you are the one sending a series of messages, you should try to help the receiver understand when you're done.

One means of doing this is using some of the many abbreviations that are common in IMs, Tweets, SMS messages, and informal e-mails. These are often initialisms (just the initials) of useful phrases that are easily recognized and save both time and keystrokes, but other shortening methods are used, too. And because there is neither body language nor voice in these media, some of these abbreviations are used to help convey attitude and tone, as well as greetings and finalization. There are thousands of abbreviations in use, so our chart on pages 78–79 has only a sampling. Check the *Painless Speaking* website for more.

ABBREVIATIONS FOR SMS, TWEETs, IMs, AND E-MAIL

Greeting

GAS	Got a second?
HIG	How's it going?
PMFI	Pardon me for interrupting
SUP	What's up?
WU	What's up?
WUZUP	What's up?
WYHAM	When you have a minute . . .

Closing/Finalization

BFN/B4N	Bye for now.
CNP	Continued in next post.
CU	See you.
CWYL	Chat with you later.
EOD	End of discussion.
EOM	End of message.
GTG	Got to go.
HAND	Have a nice day.
L8R	Later.
SIG2R	Sorry, I've got to run.
SYL	See you later.
TAFN	That's all for now.
TNT	Till next time.
TTFN	Ta ta for now.
TTYL	Talk to you later.

Interruption

BBS	Be back soon.
BRB	Be right back.
HOAS	Hold on a second.
JAM	Just a minute.
JAS	Just a second.
TBC	To be continued.
WAM	Wait a minute.

ABBREVIATIONS FOR SMS, TWEETs, IMs, AND E-MAIL, cont.	
Tone/Attitude	
404	I don't know.
AFAIK	As far as I know
AYTMTB	And you're telling me this because?
C&G	Chuckle and grin.
CMIIW/CMIW	Correct me if (I'm) wrong.
DKDC	Don't know; don't care.
DNC	Does not compute.
FWIW	For what it's worth.
FYA	For your amusement
FYI	For your information
GMTA	Great minds think alike.
ICAM	I couldn't agree more.
IDC	I don't care.
IDK	I don't know.
IHU	I hear you. (I understand/agree.)
IKR	I know, right?
IMHO	In my humble opinion
IMNSHO	In my not so humble opinion
IMO	In my opinion
JK	Just kidding.
LOL	Laughing out loud.
MEH	"Shrug"
MYOB	Mind your own business.
NBD	No big deal.
NP	No problem.
OMG	Oh my gosh!
SAT	Sorry about that.
TMI	Too much information.
WFM	Works for me.

As some of these abbreviations indicate, IM sessions can be interrupted. And not everyone bothers to set their status to clearly signal their availability or lack thereof to others. It's thoughtful to provide an accurate status, not barrage someone who's status says "here," but who may actually be away, and be ready to end a session whenever the other person has to go.

Emoticons, or smiley's, are abbreviations for facial expressions and body language and are also used to avoid misunderstandings about attitude and tone, especially when sarcasm or irony is used and the speaker's meaning is exactly the opposite of the literal meaning of the words. Scott Fahlman claims to have invented :-) and :-(in 1981, but there is also evidence that Stephen R. Cohen invented and copyrighted the smiley :) in 1984–5. In any case, they're very useful. Different apps treat emoticons differently: in some cases, they are left in text, just as they are keyboarded, but in other cases, the app will convert them into graphical images and faces. You may need to experiment to get the results you want. And, of course, knowing a range of abbreviations and emoticons will also help you interpret the messages you receive.

EMOTICONS	
Facial expression	**Meaning**
:-D	big smile
:-|	disgusted
:-<	forlorn
:-I	indifferent or angry
:-&	perplexed
:-(or 8-(or (:-(	sad
<:-o	scared
:-V	shouting
:-\	skeptical
:) or :-)	smile
:-o	surprised
:'-(	upset or crying
>8-O	very angry
;) or ;-)	wink

EMOTICONS, cont.	
Famous people/ characters/occupations	**Meaning**
=|:-)=	Abe Lincoln or Uncle Sam
O:-)	angel
d:-)	baseball player
C|:-=	Charlie Chaplin
*<:o)	clown
(8<|	Darth Vader
>:-|	Mr. Spock (*Star Trek*)
[:-|	Frankenstein's Monster
7:-)	Fred Flintstone
(_8^(|)	Homer Simpson
****:-)	Marge Simpson
*<|:-)	Santa Claus
O-)	scuba diver
Animals	**Meaning**
:=8)	baboon
' ' '^._.^' ' '	cat
***	caterpillar
8^	chicken
3:-o	cow or bull
=;=	dragonfly
6V)	elephant
>-^); > or <')))))> <	fish
- - - (8:>	mouse
3:]	pet smiley
:@)	pig
///\oo/\\\	spider
:<=	walrus

SMS text messaging and its etiquette

SMS is an abbreviation for "Short Message Service" and is also known as "text messaging." With a limit of 160 characters (in English), text messaging was not expected to be as popular as it has become, with the average cell phone user sending 357 texts per month by 2010. People use text messages as a replacement for e-mails, IMs, and phone calls. Since people who own cell phones almost always have them within reach, most text messages are delivered very soon after being sent, provided the receiver is in a spot where he or she has cell phone service. Due to the limited number of characters and the fact that there's a fee, people try to fit a whole lot into their text messages, which often include a large number of abbreviations that render common words as only one or two characters, including:

VERY SHORT ABBREVIATIONS	
Word	**Abbreviation**
and	&
are	r
at	@
ate	8
be	b
before	b4
easy	ez
for	4
from	4rm
okay	k
one	1
see	c
to, too	2
why	y
your	ur
you	u

So the message *See you before you go to eat* might look like this: *c u b4 u go 2 eat.* These abbreviations become second nature for some texters, who use them even when it's not necessary to save space. Others stick to standard English. If you pay attention to others' messages, you can be sensitive to their preferences for using or limiting the use of abbreviations.

Tweets and direct messages and their etiquette

Short (like text messages), but free (like e-mail and IMs), tweets and direct messages can be sent through Twitter from cell phones or computers but are even shorter than SMS messages, with a 140-character limit. Tweets, even if sent to an individual, can be read by anyone who cares to look at your profile or who follows you, unless you choose "Tweet Privacy" in your Twitter settings. Tweet Privacy gives you control over who follows you.

To send a private message to an individual using Twitter, you must choose what was known as a Direct Message (DM), now called a "Message" by Twitter. You can send private messages to people who follow you, and people you follow can send you private messages. So, if you're mutually following other people, you can have a private exchange. Private Twitter messages can also be sent from phones. One important characteristic of a private Twitter message is that either the sender or the receiver can delete it, and deletion makes it disappear from both accounts. This means that these messages are not a good way to convey information when you want to make sure you've got a record of it.

Besides the types of abbreviations used in other text-only formats, tweets and private Twitter messages can take advantage of URL shorteners to turn unwieldy web addresses into bite-sized chunks of alphanumeric characters.

Because most tweets are public—and by *public* we mean people throughout the world can see them—Twitter is a medium that you want to keep close control over.

Videochats and their etiquette

Videochats are similar to face-to-face conversations in some ways and different in others. Similarities include the fact that you can see each other's faces, and maybe each other's environments, and that at least some facial expressions, body language, and paralinguistic elements come through. But there are important differences. You're not in the same environment and could actually be halfway around the world from each other; you have to be seated at or carrying around your computer, phone, or tablet in order to keep the conversation going; technology difficulties can interfere with transmission or cut short the conversation; and videochats usually take some planning in order to coordinate. Because the other person can see you, unlike when you're IMing with text only, for example, it can seem impolite to multitask, so if you're going to be doing other things while videochatting, you should be sure that the other participants in your conversation are okay with that. Depending on your videochat client, you may be able to simultaneously send text messages and/or files as you chat. This way, you could, for example, share a URL and both look at the same web page or send a document file that you can then refer to together.

Audiochats and their etiquette

For those without a webcam, or when voice alone will do, there are also audiochats. Audiochats are like phone calls except that they are free and you have to stay by your computer rather than by your phone in order to keep the connection, or you may be able to audiochat via your cell phone. As with videochats, you may be able to share text or files while speaking. As with phone calls, people expect audiochats to be ongoing, unlike IMs, which may have periodic lags or interruptions, but—depending on your multitasking skills—you may be able to do something else without interrupting the conversation. Audiochats are great for meetings and catching up with friends, but possibly more interruptive and—when conducted on computers—more constraining than text messages.

Hints for choosing conversation media

With so many possibilities for conversations, it's much easier to stay in touch with other people than it used to be, and it's possible to adapt the conversation method to the type of conversation you want (or need) to have. There are methods:

- that allow you to carry on several conversations at once;
- that allow you to keep a record of the conversation;
- in which you can hear; see and hear; or use text;
- that allow you to transfer multiple types of data back and forth;
- that are more suitable for longer and shorter messages; and
- that encourage quicker or more thoughtful responses.

In addition, you may have personal preferences and so may the people you communicate with. So, rather than grabbing whatever's closest to you or seems easiest, give some thought to choosing the tool that is best for the job. And one other thing . . . just make sure you don't forget the old face-to-face method of communicating!

BRAIN TICKLERS—THE ANSWERS

Set # 8, page 47

Answers will vary. **Possible response:**
   Since I'm a writer, you might think that communicating in words would be the only type of communication I focus on. But in reality, the expression I can make through music and collage are also an important part of my communication repertoire. I value the wordless communication through color, texture, shape, and sound. Sometimes, I actually get sick of words. But eventually, I come back to them—I have to. Because for me, meaning is paramount, and words are one of the chief ways I make and receive meaning.

Set # 9, page 52

Answers will vary. **Possible responses:**

1. frankfurter, hotdog; hot cake, pancake, griddle cake; osprey, fish hawk, ossifrage

2. Native speaker of English: "Is that gouda cheese?"
   Nonnative speaker: "It's-a very good-a." (It's very good.)
   (This conversation really happened between me and a Russian immigrant.)

   Two people are talking on the phone.
   Person A: So, yeah. I'm going to knead some bread.
   Person B: How much cash do you need?
   Person A: I don't need any cash; I'm going to make wheat bread.
   (*Bread* is slang for money; *need* and *knead* are homophones.)

Set # 10, page 59

Answers will vary. **Possible lines that precede the utterance:**

1. Look, the fireworks are starting!"

2. "Watch your fingers!"

3. "I'll see you later. Have a good trip."

4. "Now isn't that just like Hugo!"

5. "The sewer backed up into my basement yesterday."

6. "I've never known Wilma to take a risk like that before."

7. "Is there any pizza left?"

8. "I saved you a seat."

9. "Did you find your stapler?"

10. "I'm going to Paris!"

Set # 11, page 60

Answers will vary. **Possible responses:**

1. Solved a riddle; verified a fact; refuted an argument; relied on an opinion about my health; explained an idea.

2. I once wrote a Tom Swifty about five times to make it as funny as possible to evoke amusement or even laughter.

Set # 12, page 73

Answers will vary. **Possible responses:**

1. Aren't you the person who won the science fair last year? I've been hoping to have a chance to ask you about your project.

2. As an eating establishment, your contribution to the food bank raffle would be especially meaningful.

3. I don't know if you remember me, but we used to play in the recreation basketball league together, and I want to speak with you about high school athletics in our state.

4. Can I help you with something?

5. I'm calling because I just saw someone cut down a tree on a national historic site.

6. I've been wondering if you could use any volunteers to help out with loading, unloading, or food preparation on Saturday afternoons.

Set # 13, page 74

Answers will vary. **Possible responses:**

1. Visiting a farm: "Could you show me how to get a duck egg out from under a duck without getting bitten?"

2. Waiting in line in the grocery store as the first week of May approaches in Vermont: "They're predicting a snowstorm this weekend, and I can't believe it!"

3. At the barbershop: "I think the new Vietnamese restaurant is really classy!"

4. Planning a date: "Do you want to go roller blading?"

5. Meeting a new acquaintance at a town celebration: "Do you remember when the town pool opened?"

6. Waiting for a plane: "Did you ever skydive?"

7. In line at the carwash: "Did you hear about the latest iPhone?"

"Once Upon a Time": Making Print Come Alive

Black marks on a white page . . . there they sit, waiting for someone to come along and bring them to life. Reading aloud and oral interpretation with a text are both rewarding ways of speaking. Using others' words, you can influence people's opinions, stir them to action, move them to tears, lead them to reassess their values. This chapter provides hints and tips for effective speaking from text.

STARTING OUT WITH TEXTS

Whether you are reading aloud or performing an oral interpretation, or even acting, you begin with written text. Sometimes you may have to perform on the spot; at other times, there's a preparation period. What do you do with this time? You've probably heard of **prewriting**—the term used to designate the planning you do as you prepare to write a text—but there's no comparable term **prereading**, even though when we read we have to

- recognize black marks on the paper as letters and words;
- process the words in groups to construct meaning and figure out how ideas are connected;
- relate the perceived meaning to what we already know about texts in general, texts of the same genre as the one we're reading, earlier information from this particular text, etc.;
- create in our minds the world of the text;
- apply prior knowledge of facts, experiences, other texts, ideas, feelings, sensory data, and the like to help us understand what we have read;
- try to recollect a new sequence of events or many facts and details; and
- fill gaps left by the text (no text tells absolutely everything that happened) with our own elaborations.

Reading aloud and oral interpretation are different from conversation because there's a text to guide you. Working with a text is a craft in itself because the skilled reader allows the many cues embedded in a text (as well as personal choices, audience, and context) to guide his or her reading. The information in this chapter will help you to get every bit of meaning from text that you can.

We'll start by examining the world of texts and different ways that they are classified, so we can use sensible categories ourselves and understand what to expect from texts that fit these categories.

We're going to assume for right now that you're working with an entire text, that is, in Bakhtin's terminology, an utterance. This is important to note because we're going to talk about the text with the assumption that it is finalized (that is, answerable), and that it completes the author's (and speaker's) desire to communicate on the given subject in the given context to a particular audience at the given time. I will use the word *utterance* interchangeably with the word *text* in this chapter. And since our focus is now on speaking, we'll use *audience* or *addressee* interchangeably to mean the one who both receives and responds to an utterance, whether the utterance is communicated in written, spoken, or signed form. To continue, we need to be able to talk about texts in a more specific way.

Classifying texts or what IS this piece of writing, anyway?

We can think about and classify texts in many different ways. I want to start by showing the limitations of some of the existing classification systems, but also how you might get some good out of them.

Classifying texts by modes of discourse

You may have learned to use a classification system that divides texts by their **mode of discourse**, categorizing them as narration, classification, description, or evaluation using one scheme and as exposition, description, narration, and argument (EDNA) using another. The modes are used as categories into which genres fit. So you may see a schema in which the mode "narration" includes works of history and biography, novels, short stories, etc. You also may have discovered the limits of these schemes by observing that not every sentence of a story or joke or anecdote is narrative. There's a whole lot of description in "narrative" speech genres, as well as sentences—or even passages—of evaluation and classification. And not every sentence of a slide travelogue is a description of a place or its features—there's often a great deal of narrative telling the history of the place. So using mode as the main way of thinking about a text we're going to read aloud is not functional.

Classifying texts by task

You may have also seen texts categorized by the overall task the author carries out. Some typical tasks are

- compare and contrast
- define or describe
- list
- narrate or record a sequence of events
- present an argument
- classify or categorize

There are two problems here. The first is the same as for the modes of discourse—the formulaic, neat answer does not match the complexity of real writing. Texts of any length generally feature multiple task types. For example, in a movie review, the author might *list* the featured actors, *classify* the movie as a comedy, tell part of the *sequence* of the plot, *argue* with another critic's analysis, and *compare and contrast* the release with the director's earlier works. In addition, the tasks usually used don't include common text elements like critique or dialogue. So using tasks as our main classification system is not useful either, although analyzing particular portions of text by the task can be very helpful.

Classifying texts by purpose

Some experts group texts by their **purpose**. They may also use the word *focus* or *aim*. Sometimes you will see categories of purpose such as *persuade, inform, express oneself,* and *entertain*.

This classification scheme doesn't work well for three reasons.

- First, it's too simplistic. We often have mixed motivations, for example persuading through humor (entertainment). And a single work may be informative in one section and persuasive in another.

- Second, the categories are too general. We might ask "persuade to do what?" or "inform to what end?" If you compare this list of four purposes with the chart of possible responses to an utterance (page 59), you'll see that it doesn't begin to describe the range of purposes an author (or speaker) might have in terms of the response.

- Third, all four purposes are expressed in terms of audience (with the author being the main audience for self-expression). If we accept Bahktin's suggestion that author, audience, speech genre, and situation or context are the four major influences on an utterance, then we have to acknowledge other types of purpose that this classification system doesn't cover. For example, in speech genres with highly defined structures, like a haiku, a major purpose is to meet the structural requirements. When giving a talk about one's work to school children as opposed to colleagues, the situation and audience will both have an impact. And being true to the subject (and the facts) is often part of the purpose in creating an utterance or—for someone who is lying—falsifying the facts in a plausible way.

SPEECH GENRES AND THEIR FIVE AREAS OF INFLUENCE

As it turns out, speech genres, both oral and written, tell us far more about a text than structure or task or purpose. They immediately give us a set of expectations about the entire utterance in five important areas: the text's typical

- structure,
- style,
- content or subject matter,
- conception of audience, and
- range of purposes.

Here is a list of some of the **main speech genres** you may find.

SOME TYPES OF SPEECH GENRES		
advertisement	folktale	parable
anecdote	gossip	play
autobiography	graduation address	poem
ballad	greeting	praise
biography	guidebook	prayer
budget	history	proposal
bylaws	interview	prospectus
case history	introduction	recipe
chronicle	invocation	report
complaint	invoice	research paper
congratulations	job application	résumé
contest entry	joke	review
contract	journal	riddle
conversation	lecture	saga
criteria	lecture notes	screenplay
diagnosis	legal brief	sermon or
dialogue	letter	homily
diary entry	manifesto	short story
dictionary	mathematical proof	song
definition	military command	speech
editorial	mission statement	state of the union
encyclopedia	monologue	summary
article	motion in a meeting	syllabus
epic	myth	tall tale
essay	news article	textbook
fairy tale	nomination	toast
farewell address	novel	user's manual
feature story	oral examination	weather report
folk song	outline	wish

A little time spent reviewing this list reveals how wide-ranging the types of speech genres are and how inadequate the modes of discourse, task, and purpose systems are for classifying them. Let's now undertake a more complete analysis.

Speech genres and structure

Some speech genres have well-defined structures that you'll recognize just from looking at their names (like dictionary definitions or recipes), while others have open structures that change with every enactment (like conversations). Structure is easiest to recognize in speech genres that have a **performative verb**. These verbs have a power over and above conveying or requesting or instructing—the verb actually enacts what it says. Saying a performative verb changes reality. Here are examples.

SOME PERFORMATIVE VERBS	
Verb	**Example Sentence**
apologize	I apologize for my behavior.
baptize	I baptize you in the name of the Father, and of the Son, and of the Holy Spirit.
bet	I bet my lilacs will bloom before May 23rd.
bless	Bless your heart!
dare	I dare you to try it.
forgive	I forgive you.
move	I so move. *or* I move that . . . . (in parliamentary procedure)
nominate	I nominate _____ for mayor.
promise	I promise to keep this secret.
pronounce	I now pronounce you man and wife.
quit	I quit!
second	I second the motion.

Some speech genres share structures. Here are examples of
how speech genres can be grouped by shared structural patterns.
Notice that speech genres used in widely differing areas of life
share similar structures.

SPEECH GENRES BY STRUCTURE	
Structure	**Examples**
Story Structure: beginning, middle, end	anecdote joke autobiography myth biography novel epic opera libretto fairy tale parable folktale play gossip short story history tall tale
Letter Structure: greeting, body, parting	business letter personal letter diary entry phone call e-mail state of the farewell address union graduation address videochat
Question-and-Answer Structure	cross-examination job interview interrogation oral examination
Argument Structure: state a proposition, offer proof	advertisement manifesto complaint mathematical diagnosis proof legal brief proposal

Not all speech genres, however, have shared structures.
Haiku, the ceremony of changing the guard, and seconding a
motion according to Robert's Rules of Order each has a unique
structure that is not shared by any other speech genre.

Speech genres and style

Some speech genres may be created in multiple styles, while some limit the range of styles (for example, some speech genres are always formal). Some speech genres allow for more individual expression on the part of the author (and speaker), while others are more restricting. Here are examples of speech genres that fit certain styles.

SPEECH GENRES BY STYLE			
Style	**Examples**		
Academic	case history		mathematical proof
	encyclopedia article		oral examination
	graduation address		reference book
	history		research paper
	lecture		syllabus
	lecture notes		textbook
Scientific	diagnosis		lab report
Technical	assembly instructions		user's manual
Artistic	autobiography	myth	poem
	biography	novel	saga
	epic	opera libretto	screenplay
	memoir	play	short story
Journalistic	editorial	news article	sports report
	feature story		
Colloquial	anecdote	joke	wish
	gossip	riddle	
Business	articles of	bylaws	job application
	incorporation	contract	mission statement
	budget	invoice	prospectus
Military	court martial record		military command
Political	party platform		state of the union
Popular/Folk	fairy tale	folktale	tall tale
	folk song	horoscope	
Religious	invocation		prayer
	parable		sermon or homily
Multiple Styles	advertisement		criteria
	blog post		diary entry
	complaint		dictionary definition
	congratulations		essay
	contest entry		farewell address
	conversation		

Speech genres and content area

Some speech genres, like conversation, can include any content in the right context and with the right participants. Others, like a medical diagnosis, allow for only a very narrow range of content. This chart shows some speech genres that can have different ranges of content.

SPEECH GENRES BY CONTENT AREA			
Speech Genres	**Examples**		
School Award Presentation	acting athletics crafts	culinary arts language music	science theatre visual arts
Event Program	athletics dance concert	festival musical opera	play variety show
Recipe	food preparation		
Lab Report	biology botany	chemistry crime	medicine physics

The New Survivors

A Collage of Images from the Holocaust

Researched and Performed by
the Students in Megan McGinley's Fifth Grade Class
Indian Hills Elementary, Salt Lake School District, SLC, Utah

2002 CHILDREN'S ARTS FESTIVAL
Soldier Hollow, Utah
May 11, 2002

The speaker's attitude toward the content (which will be revealed as the tone) also helps determine the choice of speech genre. We choose a parody, for example, to give our sarcasm an outlet, but prayers are unlikely to be sarcastic.

Speech genres and audience

Some speech genres can be adapted to suit any audience, but others are highly specialized. Bakhtin calls the speech genre's quality of being directed to someone its **addressivity**. The speech genre can distinguish the addressee by its level of formality, specificity to a certain occupation or cultural group, or applicability for a certain age. Or the addressee of a genre may be more open and unspecific. The speaker can, and should, make further choices to mold the discourse to the actual audience. As you read the chart, notice that if any of the members of

SPEECH GENRES BY AUDIENCE	
Audience	Speech Genre Examples
Young children and their parents	alphabet books fairy tales fingerplay songs folk songs nursery rhymes
Members of the armed forces	cadences military commands military instruction manuals military orders military regulations
Actors	audition announcements call back lists cue cards director's notes scripts
Executive directors of nonprofit corporations	articles of incorporation business plans bylaws employee identification number applications mission statements tax forms

the armed forces, any of the actors, or any of the executive directors also happened to be parents of infants or toddlers, we'd
have to include them in two categories.

Speech genres and purposes

The purpose in creating or speaking an utterance as Bakhtin
explains it is markedly different from the way purpose is
conceived as a classification scheme. Because the same word—
purpose—is used for both, we need to make sure we're clear on
the differences. The classification scheme—which we rejected as
simplistic, narrow, and failing to account for the range of influences on a text—allowed for only four purposes. When we talk
about purpose from here on, we will be referring to the author's
or speaker's specific goals in relation to evoking a particular type
of response from the audience. The responses an author or
speaker may seek include all those listed on page 59 and more.

We may find it useful to group these many responses by how
we want our audience to react. We may want our audience to

- **act** in a certain way
- **feel** a certain way
- **commit to** or **value** something
- **think** about or **consider** something

We can also relate these four categories of responses to speech
genres that might be used to evoke them. In some cases, a
speech genre may only work for one category of response. For
example, an actor's cue card is designed to get the author to act
in a certain way, that is, speak the words of his or her next line.
That's it. An election ballot has a similarly limited function: it's
meant to get you to respond by voting. Other genres, like novels
and conversations, can evoke a broader range of responses.
They may be crafted to elicit any category of response or even
multiple types of responses. For example, a novelist may want
you to feel for the hero of his or her story as you follow the
hero's trials and tribulations, but also to think about the values
that the hero embodies.

Now that we have the idea of response categories, we can
also relate them to particular speech genres, although some
speech genres may be able to elicit multiple responses. Of
course, this is not an exhaustive list.

SPEECH GENRES BY PURPOSE		
Purpose of Response Is to Move Audience to:	**Responses**	**Speech Genres**
Act	apply it arrange it build it buy it discuss it execute it explain it integrate it practice it produce it quote it supplement it support it teach it translate it use it	advertisement business letter business plan complaint contract graduation address guidebook instruction manual lecture manifesto military command mission statement nomination play proposal prospectus recipe sermon or homily textbook
Feel	feel any of the feelings mentioned in the chart on page 69	anecdote ballad blessing congratulations curse diary entry feature story gossip greeting haiku joke limerick novel play

SPEECH GENRES BY PURPOSE, cont.		
Purpose of Response Is to Move Audience to:	**Responses**	**Speech Genres**
Feel		praise screenplay short story song tall tale toast wish
Commit/ Value	affirm it believe it presuppose it rely on it select it	manifesto oath prayer prospectus sermon or homily testimony
Think	analyze it appraise it assess it build on it categorize it consider it criticize it demonstrate it develop it evaluate it examine it investigate it prove it rank it reinterpret it relate it to other things reorganize it solve it summarize it verify it weigh it	criteria dictionary definition editorial encyclopedia article essay history lecture mathematical proof oral examination research paper review textbook

BRAIN TICKLERS
Set # 14

The following are not complete utterances. So first you will have to guess the speech genre from which each might come. Next, give your best shot at identifying the style, content area, audience, and purpose. For 5, read the instructions and imagine how the dialogue takes place.

1. In 1900, colleges in the United States awarded 400 graduates with doctorate degrees. In 1994, more than 40,000 doctorates were granted. In the following year, 1994–1995, 65.1 million students were enrolled in schools and colleges in the United States, and in the country, an estimated $509 billion was spent on education for that school year.

2. Calico, with a lop-sided, black stripe down her nose, Sheba is my favorite of our pets. You would love her. She has long soft fur, and a sweet way of mewing to get attention if she has no more food left in her dish or wants to go out. But watch out for her temper! There's a sharp claw alert out in *this* neighborhood when Sheba's riled!

3. Dear Diary,

Dinner last night was a fiasco. As the saying goes, everything that could possibly go wrong . . . And I wanted *so* much for it to go well! How was I to know that Jeff had broken the box for the cornstarch and put it in the flour container? When I said I hoped I'd impress my guests, I didn't mean negatively.

Well, you might say, fortunately tomorrow is another day. Yes, I'd reply—the day I have a big Japanese exam. So I'd better say "sayonara."
Jenny

4. That on the first day of January, in the year of our Lord one thousand eight hundred and sixty-three, all persons held as slaves within any state or designated part of a state, the people whereof shall then be in rebellion against the United States, shall be then, thenceforward, and forever, free; and the Executive government of the United States, including the military and naval authority thereof, will recognize and maintain the freedom of such persons, and will do no act or acts to repress such persons, or any of them, in any efforts they may make for their actual freedom.

5. Instructions: Repeat what I say, but for the last syllable, say *key* instead of *lock.*

"I am a gold lock."
"I am a silver lock."
"I am a brass lock."
"I am a lead lock."
"I am a monk lock."

(Answers are on page 155.)

HOW TEXTS MAKE MEANING

Now that we've got some ideas about texts overall—we know about genre, structure, style, content, audience, and purpose, and we've looked at modes of discourse and tasks—where do we go from here? Presumably, after all this analysis, we've developed some fairly substantial ideas about meaning (for further thoughts on meaning analysis for four kinds of newspaper articles, see page 143; reports and personal essays, see page 144; stories/fiction, see page 146; scripts, see page 150; poetry, see page 152). So now we can narrow our focus to examine structure—how the writer has put the text together. The construction of texts abound with meaning cues. And the more you understand about it, the more you'll be able to bring the text meaning to life with your voice.

Every text of any length has an internal organization that may include chapters, sections, paragraphs, or stanzas. Within those divisions, sentences are sequenced, and words are ordered within sentences. Words themselves are structured from roots, prefixes, and suffixes. Through all these levels of structure and the way they are indicated on the page, the text's meaning is revealed and its performance is cued.

Orthography

Some things we gather from **orthography**, the representation of the words on the page in print. A key use of spelling is to guide us in pronunciation. We may also gather what dialect the speaker is using. In this passage from *The Pickwick Papers*, British author Charles Dickens uses orthography to represent Samuel Weller's Cockney accent:

"It won't do, Job Trotter," said Sam, "Come! None o' that 'ere nonsense. You ain't so wery 'ansome that you can afford to throw away many o' your good looks. Bring them 'ere eyes o' yourn back into their proper places, or I'll knock 'em out of your head. D'ye hear?"

The apostrophes show the dropped *th* from the beginning of the words *there* and *them* and the *f* left off the end of *of*. Dickens also shows Sam's colloquial contractions (*ain't* and *D'ye*) and the substitution of the sound /v/ for /w/.

In this poem by poet Robert Burns, we see an example of the Scottish dialect.

To a Mouse, on Turning up Her Nest with the Plough, November, 1785 (excerpt)

1   Wee, sleeket, cowrin, tim'rous beastie,
2   Oh, what a panic's in thy breastie!
3   Thou need na start awa sae hasty
4   Wi' bickerin brattle!
5   I wad be laith to rin an' chase thee
6   Wi' murd'ring pattle!
7   I'm truly sorry man's dominion
8   Has broken Nature's social union,
9   An' justifies that ill opinion
10   Which makes thee startle
11   At me, thy poor earth-born companion,
12   An' fellow-mortal!

Again, the apostrophe is used to represent omitted sounds. We can also identify lexical differences—*na* where English speakers from the United States would say *not*, *awa* where we would say *away*, *sae* where we would say *so*, etc.

In her novel *Little Women*, Louisa May Alcott uses orthography to show the pronunciation of Friedrich Bhaer, whose first language is German and who speaks English as a second language.

"At efening I shall gif a little lesson with much gladness; for, look you, Mees Marsch, I haf this debt to pay," and he pointed to my work. " 'Yes' they say to one another, these so kind ladies, 'he is a stupid old fellow; he will see not what we do; he will never opserve that his sock heels go not in holes any more, he will think his buttons grow out new when they fall, and believe that strings make theirselves.' Ah! but I haf an eye, and I se much. I haf a heart, and I feel the thanks for this."

Alcott substitutes *f* for *v* and *p* for *b* to show Bhaer's pronunciation of English and shows how he says "Miss March" by the spelling of the vowel sound in the first word and the final consonant sound in the second.

Typography

The choices made about type—including the font, size, and style—are called **typography**. A **font** is a set of designs of the upper- and lowercase letters, the numbers, and other symbols. Here are partial sets of two fonts, ITC Century above and Futura below:

ABCDEFGHIJKLMNOPQRSTUVWXYZabcdefghijklmnopqrstuvwxyz
ABCDEFGHIJKLMNOPQRSTUVWXYZabcdefghijklmnopqrstuvwxyz

Serif fonts like ITC Century have little lines at the ends of letter strokes called *serifs*. Sans serif fonts are those with lines that end plainly, like Futura. Fonts are used to differentiate elements of a text. Headings are generally set in a different font than the main part of the text (the body). In this book, the headings are Futura and the body is ITC Century.

Specialized fonts can be used to give character to certain words and suggest tone, as this set of distinctive fonts shows. But in materials that have a range of tones and styles, like novels and textbooks, plain fonts are often used. Sometimes the

- Alleycat is a playful font.
- Times New Roman is a standard, respectable serif font.
- Geneva is a plain, no-nonsense sans serif font.
- Sand is a casual font.
- Lucida Calligraphy is a sophisticated, elegant font.
- Chiledo Dos has ethnic character.
- FAJITA HAS CHARACTER, TOO.

first letter or word of a section is set in larger, specially styled type to fit a particular page design, without suggesting that this word has special importance.

Most of the body of a text is usually set in roman style, like the type you are reading now. Two other styles of type are often used. *Italic type looks like this*. It has a slight slant to the right. **Boldface type looks like this**. It has thicker lines so that the letters stand out. ***Boldface italic*** exists, but it is used less often. Boldface and italic type are often used for words that require special emphasis or to single out words that are being defined, that appear in a glossary, or that have particular importance in the text. We may signal this emphasis with our voices by slowing down and speaking the marked word(s) with special intensity, pausing before and after, and changing the pitch.

Italic style type has several other common uses. It is used to set off certain kinds of titles (books, movies, plays, television series, court cases, long musical selections, newspapers, and periodicals), as well as for the names of vessels, airplanes, spacecraft, and trains; the taxonomic names of genera, species, and varieties; letters; and words referred to as words ("the word *giraffe*").

Capitalization is another typographical means of drawing attention to single words or short phrases, a way of indicating that the word is important and should be stressed. If it is used for longer passages, as in the novel *A Prayer for Owen Meany*, this is an indication that the writer has created a unique usage, and you will need to develop an interpretation on a case-by-case basis. Here is an example of capitalization and italics, both used for emphasis in *The Crisis* Number I by Thomas Paine, December 23, 1776.

> Britain, with an army to enforce her tyranny, has declared that she has a right (*not only to* TAX) but "*to* BIND *us in* ALL CASES WHATSOEVER," and if *being bound in that manner*, is not slavery, then is there not such a thing as slavery upon earth. Even the expression is impious, so unlimited a power can belong only to GOD.

Headings and other text divisions

Headings combine typographic and content clues to help us understand the organization of the text and the relative importance of material. In a well-structured text, headings follow a consistent pattern from most important to least important. The pattern may include size, color, typeface, capitalized or lowercase letters, and placement (at the left margin, centered, indented, etc.). When reading aloud, it is usual to pause before a new heading and speak it as an announcement of what is to follow.

The **size** of a font is often used to indicate importance. The largest heading is usually the chapter title. The largest divisions within each chapter are shown by **subheads**. Divisions within a subhead are indicated by **sub-subheads**. There may be several levels of sub-subheads, the final level being **side heads**, which are run into the text, either beginning at the left margin or using a paragraph indentation, as in the following line:

Side heads. This is an example of how side heads look.

BRAIN TICKLERS
Set # 15

Make a list of the heads in Chapter 2 of this book, indicating their level and how you can identify each level.

(Answers are on pages 156–157.)

Space

Space is a design element used to give pages a pleasing, uncluttered appearance that is balanced and easy to look at. Space is also used to separate chapters, sections, and paragraphs of text. The separations help to reveal underlying organization and signal changes in content type. Space on the page is often best reflected in a pause in our reading of the text—a short "breather" to establish the change—whatever it is. In certain genres (e.g., advertisements, plays, fiction, and poetry), space may indicate pauses in the action and/or the passage of time, or have other meanings.

THINK BIG

Punctuation

Punctuation gives us a great deal of information that we can translate into reading choices. One of the reasons we can learn so much from punctuation is that it has three different roles:

- Punctuation is used to add back some of the **paralinguistic elements** we lose when we move from speech to text, including pitch, silence, stress, and tone.
- Punctuation also helps reveal **grammatical structures** by, for example, separating the distinct parts of sentences (e.g., a dependent clause from an independent clause) or marking the boundaries between two independent clauses to establish their relationship.
- Punctuation is also used to convey **semantics**—or meanings. For example, a colon between two sentence parts can indicate that the second is a further explanation of the first (Mike can't attend the party: he's in South Korea.)

While some punctuation, like commas, serve a wide range of uses, some punctuation can be understood in a meaningful way without even knowing what the words are.

EASY TO RECOGNIZE PUNCTUATION MEANINGS	
Example	**Meaning**
Word word (word word) word. Word word—word word—word.	Parenthetical material
Word word word	Omitted material *or* Passage of time
"Word word word," word word.	Quotation
Word, word, word word word word. Word; word word; word word word.	Series

But not all uses of punctuation are so obvious, and in many cases you may have to do some analysis to understand exactly what use the punctuation is serving. In addition, different authors use punctuation differently, and some are more skillful than others in using punctuation in meaningful ways, so careful attention may be needed.

Here's a brief survey of the most frequently used types of punctuation and how they might guide your decisions about how to use your voice in reading. We'll start with end marks, then move on to the types of punctuation that are likely to lead a reader to pause within a sentence, and then discuss apostrophes, quotation marks, and accent marks, more properly called *diacritical marks*.

End marks (periods, question marks, and exclamation points) separate sentences. Remember that a sentence is not a complete thought unless it is also an utterance. Usually, a sentence is only a part of an utterance, and therefore has important connections with the material that comes before and after it. These connections will help guide you in knowing how you should connect the sentences vocally.

In spite of connections, end marks usually indicate a place to pause and to breathe, though if you were reading a series of short sentences, you would likely not breathe after each one. Pauses are discussed in more detail beginning on page 130. Besides a pause, end marks often lead to a pitch shift because we tend to raise pitch at the end of questions and lower it at the end of statements. Exclamatory sentences may be raised or lowered at the end, depending on the content.

If what you are reading is a script, a short story, or a novel, you must be aware of utterance on two levels: the entire text that you have (which could be hundreds of pages)—the author's utterance—and an utterance within the world of the text, for example a speech by one character in a play or a bit of dialogue by one character in a short story.

Pauses within sentences are indicated by the marks in the bullet list that follows on the next page. You may remember that Stanislavski identified three types of pauses: logical, psychological, and breath pauses. Recently, researchers found that readers tend to coordinate their breaths with punctuation, removing breath pauses as a separate category (J. E. Huber, M. Darling, and E. J. Francis, "Influence of punctuation and syntax on breath patterns in reading." 2008, March). Good readers look ahead to identify pauses indicated by punctuation with which they can coordinate a breath. That is, rather than breathing in any old place, a skilled reader will take advantage of a pause indicated by a punctuation mark, preferring to match breaths with the most important boundaries. Many pauses are followed by a pitch shift to help the listener understand the change.

- **Ellipsis points** may indicate three different things: an omission (for example, in a quotation or when a sentence trails off without being completed), a passage of time, or a pause longer than is indicated by a dash.
- **Parentheses** or pairs of **em dashes** mark material that has the least connection to the rest of the text.
- A single **em dash** shows a change in sentence construction (its syntax), a turn of thought, or hesitancy.
- The **colon** says, in effect, *that is* or *for example* or *this is why* and is sometimes used in place of these words to introduce material. It is also used after the words *such as*, *namely, as follows*, or *for instance*. Sometimes a colon introduces a list, sometimes a complete sentence.
- Even though the **semicolon**, like the comma, has the basic meaning of addition (and), it indicates a more significant break than a comma and a longer pause in reading. If one or more items in a series contain commas, semicolons are often used to separate the items to keep the meaning clear.
- The **comma** is the (almost) all-purpose, low-key punctuation mark to show the relationship between words, phrases, and clauses. The length of the pause depends on the particular function the comma is carrying out.

Many pauses are followed by a pitch shift to indicate to the listener that there's been a change.

Apostrophes signal **elision**, the omission of a syllable by dropping it or slurring it into the next syllable. (You saw examples of this on pages 106–107 to show dialect.) This is explicit information about how to voice the text.

Double quotation marks indicate that the words of a person or character other than the text's author, narrator, or speaker are being included, shifting us into characterization (our decisions about intonation when we see this will rest on how carefully we have been able to identify that person or character). They can also indicate irony by indicating a contrast between what is said and what is meant (e.g., He said he'd help me when he has some "spare" time—might be read as, He'll never make time to help me.).

Single quotation marks are used for quotations within quotations and may also be used to indicate irony (standing for *so-called*), usually indicated by an increase in intensity, an introductory pause to gather attention, and a pitch shift.

The symbols called **diacritical marks** inform us about pronunciation. They may signal a particular sound (like the German umlaut ¨), tell us which syllable of a word to stress, or indicate that an ordinarily silent vowel should be pronounced. This last is the function of the grave accent (`) in English, which indicates that a syllable (often –*ed*) that is usually assimilated into the previous syllable is in this case pronounced as a separate syllable. Most of the time, this is found in older poetry to make a line fit the poetic meter.

BRAIN TICKLERS
Set # 16

1. Read each scenario. Choose the punctuated sentence that you think best answers the question. Explain the function of each punctuation mark (paralinguistic, syntactic, or semantic) and tell what the punctuation mark accomplishes.

   a. Several members of a committee have been uncooperative in planning an event. Arriving unprepared, they have taken up everybody's time going over material that should have been mastered previously.

The leader of the meeting makes a comment. Which rendering gives the reader the best guide to demonstrate the leader's overwhelming frustration?

   i. Now that we've gone over that, can we get down to planning please?

   ii. Now that we've gone over that, can we get down to planning, please?

   iii. Now that we've gone over that, can we get down to planning . . . please!

(continued)

b. I have several aunts, but only one uncle. My aunt refers to her husband, whose given name is Henry, as Huck. I think my uncle is terrific. Which of the following conveys that information most clearly?

   i. My aunt, Susie, calls my uncle, Henry—the dear man!—"Huck."

   ii. My aunt Susie calls my uncle Henry the dear man Huck.

   iii. My aunt Susie calls my uncle Henry (the dear man) "Huck."

2. Read the following passages. Explain how orthography, typography, and punctuation convey meaning, and how you might translate this information into choices if you were to read each passage aloud.

  a. From *The Crisis* Number I by Thomas Paine, December 23, 1776:

These are the times that try men's souls: The summer soldier and the sunshine patriot will, in this crisis, shrink from the service of his country; but he that stands it NOW, deserves the love and thanks of man and woman. Tyranny, like hell, is not easily conquered; yet we have this consolation with us, that the harder the conflict, the more glorious the triumph. What we obtain too cheap, we esteem too lightly: 'Tis dearness only that gives every thing its value. Heaven knows how to put a proper price upon its goods; and it would be strange indeed, if so celestial an article as FREEDOM should not be highly rated. Britain, with an army to enforce her tyranny, has declared that she has a right (*not only to* TAX) but "*to* BIND *us in* ALL CASES WHATSOEVER," and if being bound in that manner, is not slavery, then is there not such a thing as slavery upon earth. Even the expression is impious, so unlimited a power can belong only to GOD.

(continued)

b. From "The Purloined Letter" by Edgar Allan Poe, 1845:

Note: The Prefect of the Parisian police, Monsieur G——, has come to visit detective C. Auguste Dupin and Dupin's friend, the narrator. His case is going badly.

At length I said,—

"Well, but G——, what of the purloined letter? I presume you have at last made up your mind that there is no such thing as overreaching the Minister?"

"Confound him, say I—yes; I made the re-examination, however, as Dupin suggested—but it was all labour lost, as I knew it would be."

"How much was the reward offered, did you say?" asked Dupin.

"Why, a very great deal—a very liberal reward—I don't like to say how much, precisely; but one thing I will say, that I wouldn't mind giving my individual cheque for fifty thousand francs to anyone who could obtain me that letter. The fact is, it is becoming of more and more importance every day; and the reward has been lately doubled. If it were trebled, however, I could do no more than I have done."

"Why, yes," said Dupin, drawlingly, between the whiffs of his meerschaum, "I really—think, G——, you have not exerted yourself—to the utmost in this matter. You might—do a little more, I think, eh?"

"How?—in what way?"

"Why—puff, puff—you might—puff, puff—employ counsel in the matter, eh?—puff, puff, puff. . . ."

"But," said the Prefect, a little discomposed, "I am perfectly willing to take advice, and to pay for it. I would really give fifty thousand francs to any who would aid me in the matter."

(continued)

"In that case," replied Dupin, opening a drawer, and producing a cheque-book "you may as well fill me up a cheque for the amount mentioned. When you have signed it, I will hand you the letter."

I was astounded. The Prefect appeared absolutely thunderstricken. For some minutes he remained speechless and motionless, looking incredulously at my friend with open mouth, and eyes that seemed starting from their sockets; then, apparently recovering himself in some measure, he seized a pen, and after several pauses and vacant stares, finally filled up and signed a cheque for fifty thousand francs, and handed it across the table to Dupin. The latter examined it carefully and deposited it in his pocket-book; then, unlocking an escritoire, took thence a letter and gave it to the Prefect. This functionary grasped it in a perfect agony of joy, opened it with a trembling hand, cast a rapid glance at its contents, and then scrambling and struggling to the door, rushed at length unceremoniously from the room and from the house, without having uttered a syllable since Dupin had requested him to fill up the cheque.

(Answers are on pages 157–158.)

Extra material (footnotes, appendices, glossaries, etc.)

As you are reading the body of a text, you may come to cross-references that guide you to other parts of the book. Perhaps a superscript will direct you to a footnote or a parenthetical reference will direct you to the works cited page. Consider whether the thread of thought or argument will be strengthened or lost by an excursion to the referenced material when you are reading aloud.

Words and word order

Now we will turn our attention to the words themselves and what we can learn from them about how to use our voices in presenting a reading.

Word meaning is the first concern. Remember that if you are to interpret a text for others, you must first understand it thoroughly yourself. This means, for a start, knowing the words. Having a good dictionary available is important to the process, whether you choose a print version or an online dictionary. For links to online references, including dictionaries, visit the *Painless Speaking* web page at http://www.edreinvented.com/products/painless-speaking.

Word order, or **syntax**, serves many functions. For one thing, it helps bring important words to our attention. Writers may highlight words by placing them at the beginning or end of a sentence, paragraph, or text. In literary works, focusing on word placement can help us identify theme and overall meaning.

Rhetorical devices, called **tropes**, work with word placement and repetition of words to highlight meaning by helping us focus on the most important words and phrases in particular configurations. As readers conveying texts, we need to recognize when writers are using such devices so that we can bring them to the listener's attention. For more information about tropes, check out *A Handlist of Rhetorical Terms* by Richard A. Lanham.

BENDING THE RULES OF MEANING MAKING

Meaning can't always be grasped easily on the first try, but there are several reasons why this might be the case. On the one hand, there are devices that require readers to go beyond the surface, beyond the literal meaning of the words. On the other hand, some texts are mysterious to the reader or listener, not because of their complex artistry but because they were not skillfully crafted. If you come across such a text, it's likely not a good choice for reading aloud or oral interpretation unless you can (and have permission to) edit it.

For now, we're going to focus on the other kind of text, the kind that requires us to use various strategies to understand how the words work because they have a figurative, rather than literal, meaning. We are going to discuss three particular cases: common figures of speech, idioms, and irony.

Figures of speech

Figures of speech are groups of words that follow well-known, definable patterns but cannot be understood literally. They include the following:

- A **simile** uses words such as *like, as,* or *as if* to compare two things. To understand the simile, we must recognize the likeness between the two items being compared. An example of a simile is

  lonely as the large, pale moon

  Similes have to be well constructed to be effective. Many similes have been used so much that they have become clichés (as pretty as a picture; as light as a feather). This makes them ineffective unless they are being used to communicate that a character's thinking is commonplace or hackneyed. On the other hand, a simile that is too idiosyncratic may be open to misinterpretation. For example, if someone with an intense personal dislike of trees said "As hideous as a tree," other people who did not share the extreme view of trees would be unlikely to interpret the simile as the author wished.

- A **metaphor** compares two things that are largely different by saying that one is the other. The word *is* may be
used, or the comparison may be made by using an apposi-
tive, where the first item is renamed, like this:

*The landowner, a raging lion in defense of his property,
charged the trespassers.*

- **Personification** is a
type of metaphor in
which human charac-
teristics are attributed
to animals or inani-
mate objects.

an angry storm cloud

- **Hyperbole** is overstatement, exaggeration that can be
used for either positive or negative effect.

the finest hat ever to grace a head

- **Meiosis** is understatement for effect. It is the opposite of
hyperbole and is usually used for two opposite purposes,
to praise something or to belittle it. Meiosis includes
euphemism, the substitution of a neutral or inoffensive
phrase for one that is strong or offensive. Substituting
"passed away" for "die" is a common use of euphemism.
Meiosis also includes **litotes**, which expresses something
by negating its opposite. The expression

not the sharpest knife in the drawer

is an example of litotes used as critique, but you should
know that comments like this about someone's intelligence will be considered offensive by many people. An
example of litotes used for praise is

Hey, this is not a bad party.

By using litotes the party is commended in an
understated way.

Idioms

Idioms are like figures of speech in that you cannot infer the meaning from the literal meaning of the individual words. But they differ from figures of speech in two ways. First, they don't have defined patterns like some of the figures of speech do, and second, unlike the figures, where you can work out the meaning and are expected to do so, idioms are often unintelligible unless you already know what they mean. For example, it would be very difficult for someone who had never heard the term to figure out that *raining cats and dogs* means "raining heavily" or *kick the bucket* means "die." Here are some other examples that illustrate how differently idioms may be constructed.

SAMPLE IDIOMS	
Idiom	**Meaning**
a dog's chance	a very small chance
apple pie order	careful neatness
for the birds	worthless, unacceptable
wrote the book on x	knows all there is to know about x
get a kick out of	enjoy or appreciate

Some linguists think that idioms started as metaphors and then became set in stone (to use an idiom). Idioms can become clichés through overuse. As a speaker, you need to understand idioms in order to interpret them for your listeners.

Irony

Irony comes from a Greek word meaning "someone who hides under a false appearance." When irony is used, things appear different, even the opposite, of what they really are; unexpected events happen; what people say is not what they mean. Authors use irony to create interest or surprise, or to forge an understanding with their readers that the characters do not share. There are commonly said to be three main types of irony.

Verbal irony is irony in the use of language. It means that what is said is different from, or the opposite of, what is meant, and tone of voice is the main cue. An example of verbal irony is someone saying "Oh, great!" disgustedly when missing a bus.

In **dramatic irony**, there is knowledge that the narrator makes available to the reader that the characters don't know about. In comics and superhero movies, for example, the audience often is let in on the superhero's alternate identity, which the other characters don't know.

Situational irony can affect either a character or the reader when something that is expected with great certainty doesn't happen. A character can also face situational irony when what happens is strikingly different from what is intended. When Dorothy throws a bucket of water in the movie version of *The Wizard of Oz*, she intends only the save the Scarecrow. Ironically, this act rids the Land of Oz from the Wicked Witch of the West and helps her obtain the broomstick that she has been unsuccessfully trying to get.

BRAIN TICKLERS
Set # 17

Read this excerpt from Benjamin Franklin's satirical essay "RULES by which a Great Empire may be Reduced to a Small One: Presented to a Late Minister, when He Entered Upon His Administration" (from *The Public Advertiser*, September 8, 1773). Note the use Franklin makes of typography, orthography, punctuation, figurative language, idioms, irony, and any other patterns you see. Speak the excerpt aloud so as to give it the most meaning.

An ancient Sage valued himself upon this, that tho' he could not fiddle, he knew how to make a *great City* of a *little* one. The Science that I, a modern Simpleton, am about to communicate is the very reverse.

I address myself to all Ministers who have the Management of extensive

(continued)

Dominions, which from their very Greatness are become trouble-some to govern, because the Multiplicity of their Affairs leaves no Time for *fiddling*.

I. In the first Place, Gentlemen, you are to consider, that a great Empire, like a great Cake, is most easily diminished at the Edges. Turn your Attention therefore first to your remotest Provinces; that as you get rid of them, the next may follow in Order.

II. That the Possibility of this Separation may always exist, take special Care the Provinces are never incorporated with the Mother Country, that they do not enjoy the same common Rights, the same Privileges in Commerce, and that they are governed by *severer* Laws, all of *your enacting*, without allowing them any Share in the Choice of the Legislators. By carefully making and preserving such Distinctions, you will (to keep to my Simile of the Cake) act like a wise Gingerbread Baker, who, to facilitate a Division, cuts his Dough half through in those Places, where, when bak'd, he would have it *broken to Pieces*.

III. These remote Provinces have perhaps been acquired, pur-chas'd, or conquer'd, at the *sole Expence* of the Settlers or their Ancestors, without the Aid of the Mother Country. If this should happen to increase her *Strength* by their growing Numbers ready to join in her Wars, her *Commerce* by their growing Demand for her Manufactures, or her *Naval Power* by greater Employment for her Ships and Seamen, they may probably suppose some Merit in this, and that it entitles them to some Favour; you are therefore to *forget it all*, or resent it as if they had done you Injury. If they hap-pen to be zealous Whigs, Friends of Liberty, nurtur'd in Revolution Principles, *remember all that* to their Prejudice, and contrive to pun-ish it: For such Principles, after a Revolution is thoroughly estab-lished, are of *no more Use*, they are even *odious* and *abominable*.

IV. However peaceably your Colonies have submitted to your Government, shewn their Affection to your Interest, and patiently borne their Grievances, you are to *suppose* them always inclined to revolt, and treat them accordingly. Quarter Troops among them, who by their Insolence may *provoke* the rising of Mobs, and by their Bullets and Bayonets *suppress* them. By this Means, like the Husband who uses his Wife ill *from Suspicion*, you may in Time convert your *Suspicions* into *Realities*.

(Answers are on pages 158–159.)

MAKING DECISIONS ABOUT STRESSES AND PAUSES

So far in this chapter, we've mentioned stresses and pauses a number of times, but primarily in terms of the typographical signals we find in the text. Now we're going to focus on sentences that don't have such obvious signals.

Using stress

Stress, you may recall, is the little extra emphasis that you can give to words to draw listeners' attention to them. We do this to help listeners understand which words are most important and to help our audiences make connections and follow the flow of ideas. In reading prose, we often stress:

- important words like the subject and the verb;
- words that the writer has privileged by putting them first or last in a phrase, clause, sentence, or paragraph, or by repeating them for effect;
- words that create connections between sentences, like a noun that will be referred to by a pronoun in the next sentence;
- words that provide transitions, like conjunctions, especially those that show contrast, like *but, however, although, in spite of,* etc.;
- words that might be construed in multiple ways. There are some groups of words that can have quite different meanings, depending on where the emphasis is placed. When written, these words may be open to multiple interpretations, but a speaker has to choose which word or words to stress in order to provide an interpretation for the audience. The words *I love you,* for example, can be used to express a number of different meanings, depending on the emphasis used, as H. Wesley Balk, author of *Performing Power: A New Approach for the Singer-Actor* (University of Minnesota Press, 1986, p. 113), demonstrated in a chart, from which the following is drawn.

| MEANINGS OF "I LOVE YOU" ||
How It's Said	What It Means
I love you.	Unstressed, the basic verbal meaning is that the speaker has deep feelings for the person being addressed.
I love you.	I care enormously for you, even if someone else doesn't.

I *love* you.	Either a clarification that my feelings for you are deeper than you may ever have imagined or a contrast to someone else who only likes you.
I love *you*.	I love you, too (in response to someone who has just said "I love you").
I love *you*.	Either a response to someone who has just said "I love you" or suggesting that the relationship is one-sided (i.e., I don't think you love me).
To which we might add:	
I . . . *love you*.	A moment of revelation—I didn't realize it until just now.

- keywords for the genre ("*Once upon a time*, there was a"), purpose ("*Act* now to . . ."), or task ("How do the latest eBook readers *compare*?").

Identifying task words

Earlier in the chapter we looked at task categories that have often been assigned to whole works and decided that they were often better suited to describing portions of a work. The tasks we listed were compare and contrast, define or describe, list, narrate or record a sequence of events, present an argument, classify or categorize, critique, and present dialogue. Here, we're going to focus on the first six, because they each have a number of keywords associated with them.

TASK KEYWORDS		
Compare/Contrast		
Compare	resemble	different than
alike	same as	even though
also	similar to	however
as well as	similarly	instead
both		nevertheless
equally	**Contrast**	on the contrary
in common	although	on the one hand
in the same way	as opposed to	on the other hand
like	at the same time	still
likewise	but	though
neither—nor	conversely	whereas
not only—but also	differ	while
regardless	different from	yet
Define/Describe		
a kind of	feature	made up of
an example of	feels like	part of
antonym	for example	size
attribute	for instance	shape
category	function	smells like
characteristic	includes	sounds like
connote	illustrates	such as
contains	incorporates	synonym
defined	is	tastes like
denote	is called	type of
e.g.	is referred to as	which is
environment	looks like	whole/part

TASK KEYWORDS, cont.

List

also	as well as	in addition
and	besides	including
another	furthermore	too

Narrate or Record a Sequence

afterwards	first, second . . .	once upon a time
because	following	previously
before	history	since
cause	if . . . then	soon
consequently	last	subsequently
earlier	later	then
effect	meanwhile	therefore
finally	now	to begin with

Present an Argument

as a result	if . . . then	reason
because	nevertheless	so that
claim	notwithstanding	support
data	owing to	theory
due to	premise	therefore
even though	prove	thesis
fact	quote	

Categorize/Classify

category	heterogeneous	section
characteristics	homogenous	sort
criteria	hybrid	species
description	kind	standard style
division	manner	subdivision
family	mixed	subset
feature	order	tier
genre	phylum	trait
genus	property	type
grade	quality	variety
group	rank	

Using context to determine word stress

The importance of the particular words in the particular sentence you are going to read is determined by the **context** of the sentence. Questions like these may prove helpful in deciding which words to stress.

- What's already understood by all parties?
- What information is new?
- Of the new information, what is most crucial?
- How does the new information link to what's known?
- What relationships among thoughts, ideas, and concepts are being conveyed?
- What is the subtext?

Also consider whether you should stress more than one word, and how you might combine stress with other vocal techniques (pausing, pitch change, etc.) to create the effects you seek. And always consider the sentence in the context of the entire utterance.

Look at how the context shifts in this dialogue between a king (K) and a queen (Q), calling to each other across their royal apartment. As the context changes, notice how the queen changes the words she emphasizes.

K: Is the money under the stove?

Q: No, it's under the *dresser*.

K: I said, "Is the money under the stove?"

Q: No, the *crown jewels* are under the *stove*; the *money* is under the *dresser*.

K: Did you say the money is on the dresser?

Q: No, the money is not *on* the dresser; the money is *under* the dresser.

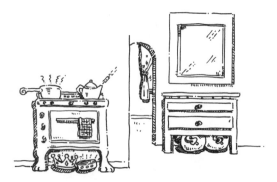

The absolutely most essential word in the last sentence is the preposition *under*. We can assume that (finally) in the context in which the last utterance was made, *money* and *dresser* were already understood by both parties. The essential information that was not yet shared between them was the exact relationship of the money to the dresser, which is conveyed by the preposition *under*.

The kind of stress in this final sentence is called **contrastive stress**: two (or more) elements are being set against each other, and so each receives vocal stress. **Additive stress** refers to items that are being compared.

BRAIN TICKLERS
Set # 18

Identify the words that should be stressed in each sentence. Find a way to say each of these sentences so that the meaning is clear. The last one is a real challenge!

1. The turnips were not on the table, but in the bathtub.
2. The turnips were not stacked on the table, but piled in the bathtub.
3. The turnips were both piled in the bathtub and stashed in the linen cupboard.
4. The chickens were neither white nor brown.
5. The chickens were neither white nor brown, but a delicate shade of lavender.
6. "In the progress of politics, as in the common occurrences of life, we are not only apt to forget the ground we have traveled over, but frequently neglect to gather up experience as we go." *The Crisis* Number III, Thomas Paine.
7. "Those who expect to reap the blessings of freedom, must, like men, undergo the fatigues of supporting it." *The Crisis* Number IV, Thomas Paine

(continued)

8. "There is a dignity in the warm passions of a whig, which is never to be found in the cold malice of a tory." *The Crisis Number VI*, Thomas Paine

9. "It is not a little remarkable that in every case reported by ancient history in which government has been established with deliberation and consent, the task of framing it has not been committed to an assembly of men, but has been performed by some individual citizen of preeminent wisdom and approved integrity." *Federalist Paper No. 38*, Madison

10. I didn't say to meet at the green house: I said, "Meet me at the greenhouse!"

(Answers are on pages 159–160.)

Using pauses

Constantin Stanislavski, in his work *Building a Character*, emphasizes the importance of the pause in speech by comparing the two sentences illustrated below.

Pardon—impossible
send to Siberia.

Pardon impossible—
send to Siberia.

Of course, not every pause a speaker makes will be this important, but it is a good idea to note the pauses suggested by paralinguistic elements, grammatical structures, and semantics (the three kinds of pauses indicated by punctuation) and to consider how exactly you will convey them as logical or psychological pauses. Ask yourself the following questions:

- How long will I pause?
- What do I mean to convey by the pause—hesitation, fear, anger, frustration, desire that someone else speak first, a pause for a character to get thoughts straight, an inability to speak due to an overwhelming flood of emotion, or something else?
- I will not be speaking, but what will I be doing? Will I look up at my listeners? Will I breathe during the pause? Will I gesture? Will I move?
- H. Wesley Balk in *Performing Power: A New Approach for the Singer-Actor* gives a list of possible meanings for what he refers to as the **tactical pause**: "A pause can say 'I don't like what I'm going to say' or 'I *relish* what I am going to say,' or 'Listen very carefully to what I say next,' or 'Did you hear what I just said? I'm going to give you time to assimilate it,' or 'I just had an idea that stopped my previous train of thought and launched me on a new one.' The most important message, however, is the one that accompanies all the preceding examples: 'I haven't finished. Continue to pay attention, in fact pay *closer* attention!'" (p. 132).

PREPARING TO SPEAK FROM TEXT

If you are going to read aloud, present an oral interpretation, or act from a script and have a chance to prepare, then this is the place for you to pick up pointers and tips to help you through the process. If you're anticipating having to read on the spot with no preparation time, you'll find helpful information beginning on page 226.

Of course, text is a crucial part of the reading experience, but there are three other essential elements of the reading situation: you, your audience, and the occasion.

Text and context

Let's start with you. The way you read aloud reflects who you are. Your reading is a product of your favored performance mode, the types of intelligence that are most prominent in your make up, your skills, gifts, talents, and interests. Your reading is also informed by your knowledge about texts and speech genres and by prior knowledge about the topic of the text you're reading. Your enthusiasm for reading, your past experiences reading aloud, and other things going on in your life may also have an influence on your reading. Except that they are responding, rather than performing, your audience has the same influences on their response that you do on your performance. But if there's more than one of them, you have to try to address them all at once, with their different interests, modes, and abilities. This is made easier by learning about your audience.

The occasion includes the function and purpose of the reading performance, which can be viewed from the point of view of you, the reader, your audience, and a sponsoring organization, if there is one. It also includes the setting and the available resources. Here are some questions that can help you think about your reading.

ANALYZING THE READING CONTEXT

Function for the audience
- first hearing of a text they will be tested on?
- story hour?
- public lecture they chose to attend?
- fun with an older sibling?

Function for you
- lesson for a class in public speaking?
- volunteer work for a local nursing home?
- public lecture you chose to deliver?
- fun with a younger sibling?
- forensic speech club activity?

Purpose of the reading event
- for audience?
- for you?

Possibilities and limitations
- location, e.g., classroom, home, office, theatre?
- number in audience?
- preparation time available?
- taking turns with other readers or featured performance?
- props, costumes, make-up, audiovisual aids?
- part of celebration or event?

Considering these factors will help you think about adapting your performance to be the best fit for the context.

Understanding more about your listeners

When you read aloud, interpret, or act from a script, remember that you are processing the words very differently from your audience. We reviewed the challenges of listening when we talked about orality and literacy in terms of conversation (see page 63). For example, as a listener, you can't look back to see what happened earlier—you have to rely on your memory.; it's easier to think about concrete material than abstract material; it's difficult to process a lot of complexity; and repetition and mnemonics can help with recall. To assist you to do a really fine job of preparing for and delivering aural messages, we're going to explain in more detail how speech is processed. Hearing words is different than seeing words:

- A spoken utterance is first perceived by the listener as a semicontinuous acoustic signal with breaks only when the speaker pauses. Did you ever stop to think that sound doesn't come to us divided into words and phrases, but as a stream?
- Our first task as listeners is **segmentation**—dividing the acoustic signal into recognizable sections. We simultaneously analyze the speech signal into:
  - **phonemes** (sounds);
  - **morphemes** (meaning units);
  - words;
  - phrases;
  - sentences;
  - units of discourse (like the tasks we've discussed);
  - and utterances.
- We search our mental **lexicon** (dictionary) for **phonological strings** (groups of sounds) that match what we've heard, preanalyzed into our best guess at words units. When we find a match, this brings up the **semantics** (meaning) of the word unit we've identified.
- We then use paralinguistic elements, including stress and intonation, as well as relative loudness, pitch, and duration of syllables, to help guide us in understanding the **syntactic structure** (word order) of the utterance.

This amazingly complex process is so speedy and automatic that we can do all this and prepare our own response at the same time!

What if we don't find a match for one or more phonological strings (that is, there's a word or phrase we don't understand)? In that case, we can try to use other information to refine our guess (for example, infer the word from context); we can skip it, if it doesn't seem too important to the meaning; or we can ask the speaker for assistance in interpreting.

What if the semantic and syntactic information doesn't combine into an interpretable sentence? As suggested above, we refine our guess using additional information, decide that we can do without the particular piece of the message, or ask for help.

Our awareness of this complex process can remind us to make thoughtful choices as we read aloud.

Choosing a text

If we get to choose the text we'll be reading aloud, we have these things to keep in mind: the text itself, the reader, the listener, the context, and the nature of listening and orality. Life could be really easy: you could offer to read to your little sister, and she could blurt out, "I want *Don't Tell Me a Ghost Story!*" which just happens to be a book you read over and over as a child and would love to read to her because it has really good spooky ghost noises and a ghost named Moooooooky Bloooooooky in it. In case life doesn't turn out to be so simple, follow along here for some solid guidelines.

We expect different excellencies from a story than from a letter; we hope for different enjoyment from a well-conceived essay than from a play. Because texts have different aims, we cannot make a general rule for choosing them except this: whatever they are trying to do, they should do well (unless our purpose in reading is to demonstrate their failure).

Literary critic and researcher Louise Rosenblatt noted that a reader approaches a text along a continuum, with *efferent reading* at one extreme and *aesthetic reading* at the other. **Efferent reading** focuses on the *information* to be acquired, while **aesthetic reading** focuses on the *reader's experience* during the reading event. Rosenblatt says that aesthetic reading is the special mark of the literary work of art because it is lived through by the reader. Let's turn our attention to these two types of text and how an understanding of them might affect how we choose a work to read, as well as how we present our reading of it.

Aesthetic texts

Henry David Thoreau says in *Walden,* "Could a greater miracle take place than for us to look through each other's eyes for an instant?" Books that have a story structure—fiction, autobiography, travelogues, history, and so on—can give us that view, and these are all books that we as readers, or listeners, experience aesthetically.

What is it that allows aesthetic experience to happen? It is the result of a combination of factors, one of the most important being that the text is so unified and coherent that nothing within the text knocks you outside the world of the story. "Willing suspension of disbelief" is the name that poet Samuel Taylor Coleridge gave to what we do when we temporarily give up the world of reality and enter the world of aesthetic experience. J. R. R. Tolkien says in his essay "Tree and Leaf," ". . . the story-maker . . . makes a Secondary World which your mind can enter. Inside it, what he relates is 'true': it accords with the laws of that world. You therefore believe it, while you are, as it were, inside. The moment disbelief arises, the spell is broken; the magic, or rather art, has failed. You are then out in the Primary [real] World again, looking at the little abortive Secondary World from out-side." So if you find a text in which

- the dialogue is unbelievable,
- the diction is inconsistent,
- the characterization is weak,
- the characters' motivations don't seem to fit,
- the plot is convoluted or wildly improbable, or
- the attitudes seem inappropriate to the characters,

put it aside and search for something with more coherence.

Literature, being art, is partially about fulfilling and denying expectations, of leading the reader/listener on a chase until a satisfying (though not necessarily happy) ending is reached. To this end look for:

- a plot that is suspenseful and interesting
- themes that resonate with what you know of life
- characters that are admirable or at least fascinating
- vivid description that evokes your imagination
- valuable insights and understandings that enrich your life
- a sense of emotional expansion from having lived through the story

Aesthetic experience also depends on the presentation. Edgar Allan Poe, in his essay "Twice-Told Tales," says that aesthetic experience happens when one experiences "totality." But totality is easily missed if "worldly interests, intervening during the pauses of perusal, modify, counteract and annul the impressions intended." So you want to be able to read uninterrupted so your listeners experience the entire utterance without pause. And—thinking about the facts we know about listening, processing, and recall—this means that you may want to choose a text with an appropriate level of vocabulary and complexity, and a memorable storyline so that your audience will not feel the need to break the spell of totality by interjecting questions.

If, however, you are reading to young children or other people who have special needs, set your sights accordingly and incorporate the conversation with your listeners as best you can into your presentation as an integral part of it, rather than viewing it as "interruptions."

Efferent texts

Unlike an aesthetic text, an efferent text should generally be as predictable as possible: every connection should be clear, and every piece of information and its relation to the whole, evident. Whereas an aesthetic piece may hope to thrill you by starting *in medias res* (in the middle of things), a well-written efferent piece should usually "begin at the beginning . . . and go on till [it] come[s] to the end: then stop," as the White King advised Alice.

In talking about textbook design in 1984 ("Content Area Textbooks" in *Learning to Read in American Schools: Basal Readers and Content Texts*, Lawrence Erlbaum Associates, Publishers, 1984), researchers Bonnie B. Armbruster and Thomas H. Anderson defined a **considerate text** as one "designed to enable the reader to gather appropriate information with minimal cognitive effort." Since all efferent texts are designed to transmit information, I propose that we can use Armbruster and Anderson's four evaluative categories—structure, coherence, unity, and audience appropriateness—to help us judge efferent texts that we are considering reading aloud or presenting as an oral interpretation.

Structure

Armbruster and Anderson say that **the topic, purpose, and structure of the text should be readily apparent from the headings and/or topic sentences.** Read through the headings of the section of text you are considering using, skipping the text in between. Does it make sense? Then read through only the first sentence of each paragraph. Can you follow along? If so, you have a well-structured text. What Armbruster and Anderson say about structure for readers is ever so much more true for listeners, who have, in most cases, no visual cues to support their memories, who cannot "look back."

Coherence

Coherence means holding together. It means that **connections in the text should be clear—both connections between and among ideas and events mentioned in the text, and connections between and among elements of the text (i.e., words, phrases, clauses, sentences).** This implies that relationships between and among ideas and events should be explicitly stated. References from one part of the text to another (e.g., pronoun references and quantifiers like *few, some, many*) should be clear. Sequences of events should move through time in one direction only.

Does the text include any portions that have the six tasks we noted: compare/contrast, define/describe, list, narrate or record a sequence, present an argument, and categorize/classify (see the chart on pages 126–127)? If so, you can check for the key words noted on the chart. Does the text use these words to make connections?

Unity

Armbruster and Anderson use *unity* to mean singularity of purpose. Unity includes whatever the writer intends to do; in Bakhtin's terms, **the text should be an utterance—no more, no less. In other words, the text should be finalized.** This can be the case only if every idea in the text contributes to the purpose—material that is ancillary to the main purpose should appear in footnotes, appendices, sidebars, or charts, not within the main body of the work. Although they do not mention it, another failure of unity would be the omission of material that is essential to the complete rendering of the writer's purpose.

Audience appropriateness

We've already talked a bit about listener characteristics such as response mode and intelligence (pages 131–132). Armbruster and Anderson speak specifically only of the **text matching the reader's (or listener's) knowledge base**. The knowledge base includes prior knowledge about speech genres that allows the reader to predict the text structure, as well as prior knowledge about the content area. If it is necessary to introduce technical terms or other difficult vocabulary, the terms should be defined clearly upon first usage, and their meanings repeated, if it seems necessary. Any use of language that cannot be literally construed— irony, idioms, or figures of speech—should be carefully considered in terms of the audience. Check analogies for clarity, too.

The amount of complexity is also a consideration. Although they raise this issue in terms of unity, Armbruster and Anderson's citation of a study by G. A. Miller in *Psychological Review* (1956), which found that short-term memory can hold only about five to nine items at one time, seems more pertinent here. Armbruster and Anderson suggest that poor and beginning readers would have more difficulty than average readers with complex text (perhaps they'd remember fewer than five items). It is not difficult to believe that inexperienced listeners or those listening to a second language might also have difficulty.

Other considerations

Also think about the following factors:

- How much time do you have to make your presentation? Is the piece a good match or will you have to cut or excerpt it? Do you have the skill and time to do so?
- Can the text you are thinking about stand on its own? Would it work with a short introduction? Or is it too complicated to use in the given time?
- Would doing an excellent job of preparation require a lot of research on your part? Do you have the time and resources to complete such research?

Pre-reading a text

It stands to reason that all those text cues that we talked about on pages 106–127 help you much more if you identify and think about them *before* you actually start reading to your audience. It's much harder to catch all the clues on the fly than it is to pick them up during a slow, thoughtful preparation time. Writer Vladimir Nabokov goes so far as to say in his lecture on "Good Readers and Good Writers," "one cannot *read* a book: one can only reread it. . . . [W]e must have time to acquaint ourselves with it. We have no physical organ . . . that takes in the whole picture . . . [until] a second, or third, or fourth reading." When we consider the complexity of the task of reading (see page 91), this point makes sense.

And how do you pre-read? The philosopher Friedrich Nietzsche would answer, "slowly." He says, in his preface to "Daybreak," "read slowly, deeply, looking cautiously before and aft, with reservations, with doors left open, with delicate eyes and fingers." This kind of thoughtful reading will help you find the clues and the patterns that will lead to the most rewarding reading experience. Here are some steps you can take:

Step 1: Identify the speech genre of a piece of text. Use the clues provided by its structure, style, content, conception of audience, and purpose. (For more detailed information on some major speech genres, see pages 94–103.)

Step 2: Go through the text and identify the tasks the writer carries out: compare/contrast, define/describe, list, narrate or record a sequence, present an argument, and categorize/classify (see page 93). Jot notes in the margin. (If the text doesn't belong to you, and you are doing a school assignment, you may be able to get permission to make a copy.)

Step 3: Go through the text and identify the writer's purpose(s) (see pages 93–94).

Step 4: Now, as closely as possible, identify the writer's audience.

You should now have a good, general idea about what kind of a text you have before you.

Marking a text

Don't assume that you'll be able to remember everything you find out about a text! Don't even try! Marking a text is an excellent way to maintain a record of your discoveries and your plans. In fact, marking a text is something you should do whenever possible because it's a good way to make a book your own. You can not only respond to the writer, narrator, speaker, and/or characters but also give yourself helpful reminders, collate information, and/or record your reactions to the unfolding of the plot or argument. Here are some helpful hints on how reading with a pen or pencil can add depth to your experience. Before you start, make a clean copy or two to use for your reading analysis. That way, you don't have to be concerned that your markings will interfere with your performance.

Book as conversation

By definition, when you read a book, you're experiencing another person—the writer—who has something to say. With pen in hand, you can speak back. Questions, comments, evaluations, even arguments are fair game. Some comments you might want to use are

- Yes/No
- !!!!! (as many as you need)
- TAT ("think about this")—for points that need pondering
- WM? ("what [does this] mean?")—for points that need clarification

Or perhaps you've already developed some notations of your own.

Memory aids

If this text is important to you, you know that you're going to want to find things again. Using underlining and margin notes can help. Here are some ideas.

- Title untitled chapters with a name that will help you recall the contents.
- On the inside front cover or first page, list items you need to find again: important quotations, appearance of symbols, page numbers of significant events or information.
- Invent a system to record the occurrence of repeated ideas, symbols, connections, themes, and other important details such as key words or important quotations in the margin.

Links/connections

As already indicated, noting places in which repetition ties one part of a book to another is important. But beyond that, sometimes a book will call up a link to another source—a reference or allusion will be known to you; a thought or quotation will connect to something someone else said or wrote. Write it in the margin. You may find the connection valuable later.

Reading instructions

Remember all those ways the text makes meaning? Marking the text is the way to call them out for yourself. You can develop a system to mark stresses, pauses, pitch shifts, changes in tone, use of character voices, and so on. Examples are provided in Appendix C.

Flag it

Self-stick flags can be really helpful. One thing you may wish to do is mark each page that begins a chapter with a numbered flag. This makes locating information much quicker than thumbing through every time. You can also color-code different topics to make your task easier.

Reading some important speech genres

Here are some guidelines for approaching the interpretation of nine different major speech genres: news stories, editorials, feature pieces, sports stories, reports, personal essays, stories or fiction, scripts, and poetry.

Newspaper articles

There are several specific subgenres within the category of newspaper articles. **News stories** are attempts at objective writing. They are front-loaded—that is, they attempt to answer the Five Ws and an H questions—Who? What? Where? When? Why? and How?—in the very first paragraph, so that readers can gather the gist of the day's news by reading the headline and first paragraph only of each of the front-page stories. There is little to "interpret" in reading a news story. Clarity and pacing to make sure that the bulk of information at the front is not overwhelming is important. There is no characterization (some news stories don't even have a byline identifying who wrote them—they simply are credited to a news wire service), and the use of intonation to show feeling is not appropriate when reading a news story as a news story.

 Editorials are persuasive pieces. Some are unattributed and are just "the voice of the paper," while others come from established editorial writers for the paper who are known for their particular views, or even for their particular biases. **Op eds** are opinion pieces by writers not employed by the newspaper—often readers or others who seek a forum for their take on things. **Feature pieces** may have some of the same topics that make the news section, but with a twist. Here there is humor, intrigue, passion. Both editorials and feature stories may be written from either the third-person or first-person point of view, but neither attempts to be objective. In reading either of these, it's important to identify the speaker, and to stick to the facts—this is not a character you're making up; this is a real, live human being. If you have the opportunity, you can read other articles or editorials by the same writer to expand your understanding of him or her.

 For an editorial writer, you want to identify his or her values and perspective. For a feature writer, you want to figure out how to make the most of this "light touch" on the news by identifying the twist the writer takes. Does the story make the news into a feature by using the grotesque, humor, the unusual, local interest, an emotional appeal, or some other approach? Where's the excitement and drama in the piece? How can you best convey that with your voice?

Many **sports stories** appeal to very narrow audiences, although you may find some that deal with larger issues and so broaden their appeal. But a story about a particular game, no matter how well written, colorful, and exciting the prose, is likely to have limited interest beyond the folks who follow the particular teams involved in the competition or maybe, depending on the level of play, the particular sport. Reading a sports story well requires knowing the jargon. You must also know the idioms and what they mean to give them appropriate intonation, and you need to know how to say the abbreviations. For example:

NCAA (National Collegiate Athletic Conference)
can be either N-C-double A or N-C-A-A
but
NESCAC (New England Small College Athletic Conference)
is /NES-kack/ not N-E-S-C-A-C

You can check with a local newspaper sports room for assistance.

Essays

You may find yourself reading aloud two distinctly different types of essays. The first is a factual, third-person, objectively written essay, which might, in some circumstances, be called a **report**. In this type of essay, the persona of the writer is usually somewhat concealed. You are not called upon, in this case, to develop characterization or a well-defined voice for the narrator. Your role here is to transmit, as clearly as possible, the information that is within the text, whether it is meant to inform, define, or explain, etc.

The factual essay's appeal will usually depend on its topic, unless—which sometimes happens—the writer uses a microcosm to draw conclusions about the world at large in the end. In either case, if you are choosing material for an older audience, a good essay, even if it's on a topic in which they previously had no interest, may draw them in. In choosing material for a young audience, you may have to think carefully to find a topic that will hold their attention.

Personal essays are always written in the first person. Though the content may be focused on a very narrow field about which the writer has personal knowledge, the theme of a personal essay is usually some universal theme that expands the view from this field to life in general.

Here are some essayists whose work you may want to read.

ESSAYISTS	
Maya Angelou	C. S. Lewis
Russell Baker	George Orwell
Sandra Cisneros	Thomas Paine
Annie Dillard	Walker Percy
Ralph Waldo Emerson	Lewis Thomas
Benjamin Franklin	Henry David Thoreau
John Hersey	James Thurber
Jamaica Kincaid	John Updike
Maxine Hong Kingston	E. B. White
William Least Heat Moon	Richard Wright

BRAIN TICKLERS
Set # 19

Find a story from a newspaper or an essay that you think would make good material for reading aloud in some context and do the following for it:

1. Define the context you think it fits.
2. Pre-read the text using the four steps on page 140.
3. Mark the text.
4. Read the text aloud, pretending to be in front of an audience.

(Answers are on page 160.)

Stories/Fiction

"My task," said writer Joseph Conrad, in the introduction to *The Nigger of the 'Narcissus': A Tale of the Sea*, "which I am trying to achieve is, by the power of the written word, to make you hear, to make you feel—it is, before all, to make you *see*. That, and no more, and it is *everything*." When you read a story to listeners, don't think of yourself as just speaking words: think of yourself, as Thoreau said, as allowing your listeners to look through another's eyes for an instant.

Imaging during reading aloud is known to unify comprehension, and the same thing happens if we use our imaginations to picture a story that we *hear*. So when you look for stories, look for stories with which you can make pictures using your voice.

Stories have a narrator, an imaginary person, invented by the writer for the purpose of telling the story. First-person narrators participate in or are eyewitnesses to the story events. Third-person narrators may be omniscient (they know everything there is to be known about the world of the story) or limited (they see only part of the world, as an individual does). The story may say explicitly who the narrator is, or it may not. But this narrator, however much or little you know about him or her, is your road into the story, because when you read the story, you take on the character of the narrator. So you need to decide how you respond to the narrator.

Another element to look at is how the story appeals to you. Good stories appeal to both the mind and the heart—they work neither entirely by logic, nor entirely by feeling. And whether it's humorous, tragic, romantic, or adventurous, a good story can broaden your understanding of what it means to be human, teach you something about life, inspire you, enrich you. So think about whether the story moves you in some way.

If it does, then you want to explore deeper and discover the story's theme, which is the story's point or its message. A theme is usually a generalization about life or human behavior or values; it is true, but not a truism; rather, it reflects the author's insight into the way things are that she or he wants to share with readers. Theme is an important part of a story's meaning and is developed throughout the story, and some stories can even have multiple themes and meanings.

Besides patterns and symbols in the story (which often point to the theme), certain parts of a story often refer fairly directly to the theme: the title, the beginning, and the very end. An important character's first and final words or thoughts are also likely to carry powerful indications of theme. These privileged places—along with the plot, the character, the setting, the mood, and the tone—all combine to create the thematic meaning of the story. The theme of a story may never be explicitly stated, but it's what the story's about, what it means.

Choosing a story is different than choosing other material because many stories can be enjoyed on a surface level without a deep understanding of theme. The "meaning" of a story may come to someone later, after time and thought, or the person may simply continue to enjoy a well-constructed plot. Because of this, stories can be chosen to fit an audience with wide-ranging backgrounds—for example, families—without as much trouble as one might at first think.

Besides fairy tales, folk tales, myths, and tall tales, short stories by the following writers may provide you with material that you do not need to excerpt in order to use it for reading aloud.

SHORT STORY WRITERS

Heinrich Böll	Jack London
Ray Bradbury	Bernard Malamud
Fray Angelico Chavez	Guy de Maupassant
Anton Chekhov	Saki
Sandra Cisneros	Isaac Bashevis Singer
Stephen Crane	Amy Tan
O. Henry	James Thurber
Langston Hughes	Anne Tyler
Shirley Jackson	Kurt Vonnegut
Ursula Le Guin	Jessamyn West

BRAIN TICKLERS
Set # 20

Find a story that you think would make good material for reading aloud and do the following for it:

1. Define the context you think would work well.
2. Pre-read the text using the four steps on page 140.
3. Mark the text.
4. Read the text aloud pretending to be in front of an audience.

(Answers are on page 160.)

Reading in a group

Sometimes reading aloud is a group activity—for example, reading a play in a literature class, doing an audition, reading a dialogue in a foreign language class, performing a reader's theatre piece, or doing a choral reading. Here are four pointers for reading with others.

1. **Follow along.** Follow along in the text while the other readers are reading. This way you won't lose your place.
2. **Pay attention to cues.** A cue is a signal to begin speaking. Your cue is the end of the line of the person speaking before you. The end of your line is the cue for the person speaking after you.
3. **Share the limelight.** Getting attention at the expense of the other performers is called **upstaging**. Learn to give and take individual focus as the main attention in the material shifts.
4. **Strive for balance.** "Freedom and Unity" is the Vermont State motto, and it's a great statement of the need to balance personal creativity and interpretation with what's going on in the rest of the group. The trick is to give the best you're capable of giving while working together to achieve a coherent whole.

There are a variety of ways to read with others. You may participate in the production of a play or musical with a director, cast, crew, and all the accoutrements. Or you may have a part in a smaller scale production such as a reader's theatre performance. Reader's theatre is defined in several different ways and is sometimes used synonymously with chamber theatre, but the main point is that it is *presentational,* not *representational.* The piece to be performed is spoken, but there is no staging to accompany the dialogue. The actors are still, and the characterization takes place in the voice, without movement, costume, or make-up. The actors face the audience, not each other. Presentations may include scripts or narratives adapted to the theatre using a narrator.

Scripts

The structure of a play is built around conflict. The action is initiated by an **inciting incident** that generally takes place before the play begins. As the play starts, **exposition** introduces the essential background information, as well as characters, situations, and conflicts. (Exposition may be found throughout the play as well as at the beginning.) At the **point of attack**, the chain of events initiated by the inciting incident disrupts the status quo, the **major conflict** of the drama is revealed, and the **rising action** begins. Tensions that occur after the major conflict has been established and that block the **protagonist** from resolving this conflict are called **complications.** At the **crisis** or **turning point**—usually the point at which the main character's action or choice determines the outcome—the outcome becomes irreversible. This moment may or may not coincide with the **climax** or **high point** of the action. The **falling action** follows, and the play concludes with the **resolution** or **denouement** when whatever is going to be wrapped up is concluded and the story is finished.

Though many older plays have five acts, there are also scripts for one-act plays, two-act plays, three-act plays, individual scenes, and (debuting in 1977 in Louisville, Kentucky, at the Humana Festival of New American Plays) the ten-minute play created by John Jory. Screenplays are characteristically written in three acts.

The conflict in a play is different than that in fiction because a play (with a few notable exceptions, like *Our Town*) has no narrator. Therefore, the conflict is shown by the words and actions of the characters—the agents of the conflict—rather than told by an observer or participant. Each speech moves the action deeper into conflict or toward resolution.

Keep in mind that most scripts are created first and foremost for full performance. When a script is presented in a simple reading—in the course of classroom work, in reader's theatre, and the like—then there will, of necessity, be elements left undeveloped. When reading a script in a classroom setting, one person should read the stage directions, a crucial element of the text. You may wish to consult an expert from a theatre department at a local college or university for more information.

You can look for plays by the following playwrights:

PLAYWRIGHTS	
Cherie Bennett	Reginald Rose
Paddy Chayefsky	William Shakespeare
Anton Chekhov	George Bernard Shaw
William Gibson	Neil Simon
José Cruz González	James Still
Barry Kornhauser	Mary Hall Surface
Brian Kral	Thorton Wilder
David Mamet	Tennessee Williams
Arthur Miller	Y York
A. A. Milne	Susan Zeder

To listen to radio plays, check the links on the *Painless Speaking* website.

BRAIN TICKLERS
Set # 21

Choose a) a play or a scene that you think would make good material for reading aloud in some context and b) enough people to read it with and do the following for it:

1. Define the context you have chosen.
2. Pre-read the text using the four steps on page 140, and then mark it.
3. Read the script aloud with your fellow actors in your chosen context.

(Answers are on page 160.)

Poetry

Poems make meaning through the order and patterning of sound. They appeal to the senses and make the most of every syllable and word. In order to work with poetry—first to select and analyze it and then to prepare it for reading aloud—you will need some facility with the key aspects of poetry: poetic structures, rhythm and meter, and sound devices, including rhyme. The speech genre of the poem is a useful starting point. You should identify the poem's structure, noting the use of stanzas (if any) and lines. If the poetry has a meter, you should identify it. It's a good idea to chart the rhyme scheme for the end rhymes, if they're used, and analyze the poems for other uses of rhyme, as well as other sound devices. See *Painless Poetry* for more information.

RHYTHM AND METER

Meter is the basic underlying pattern of stresses in the lines of a poem. If you have ever tapped your foot to music, you were tapping the meter. The **rhythm** is how the words fit into the meter in a particular poetic line. Just as in the musical meter of, say, $\frac{3}{4}$ (three beats to a measure and a quarter note gets one beat), not every measure consists of three quarter notes, similarly in poetry, not every foot—the equivalent of a note—in the line of a poem matches the poetic meter.

Poetic feet are characterized by the number of syllables they have and where the strong and weak stresses fall in them. Here is a chart of the main poetic feet in English poetry, with their names, their stress patterns, and an example for each.

POETIC FEET			
Number of Syllables	Stress on First Syllable	Stress on Last Syllable	Stress on First and Last Syllables
2	trochee strong–weak *urgent*	iamb weak–strong *persuade*	spondee strong–strong *true-blue*
3	dactyl strong–weak– weak *happily*	anapest weak–weak– strong *guarantee*	amphimacer strong–weak– strong *first and last*

SOUND DEVICES

Some sound devices are used in poetry more often than others. **Onomatopoeia** refers to words that imitate the sounds they name. Examples include *whirr, buzz, zoom, swish, zip, crackle,* and *mew*. **Euphony** means the use of smooth, flowing, harmonious sounds. Euphony often includes repeated vowel sounds and the so-called liquid consonants, *l* and *r*. **Cacophony** is the opposite of euphony, the purposeful use of harsh sounds. It often features repeated use of the sounds /k/, /ch/, /tch/, and /t/. **Voiced consonants** (*b, d, g* as in *goose, j, l, m, n, ng, r, th* as in *then, v, w, y, z,* and *zh*) and **consonant blends** (*str, wr,* etc.) take longer to say and poets use them to slow down the pace of their lines.

Rhyme is the sound device that most people are familiar with. Rhyme can be categorized by its placement and the type of sounds that are repeated. In the category of rhyme placement, there are three main categories of rhyme placement:

- **End rhyme** is rhyme at the end of lines. It is the most often used.
- **Initial rhyme** is rhyme at the beginning of lines.
- **Medial rhyme** is rhyme between a word somewhere in the middle of the line with another word, which may be in three different places:
  - If the second rhyming word is at the end of the same line, then we have **internal rhyme**.
  - If the second rhyming word is also somewhere in the middle of the same line, then we have **close rhyme**.
  - If the second rhyming word is in the middle of a line before or after the line, then we have **interlaced rhyme**.

There are also three main types of rhyme:

- **Identical rhyme** is rhyme in which the exact same word is repeated.
- **Perfect rhyme** is rhyme in which one or more syllables are repeated *except for the initial sound*. Perfect rhyme includes both *ham/jam* and *honey/bunny*, for example.

- **Near rhyme** is rhyme that doesn't meet the criteria for perfect rhyme, but has similar sounds nevertheless, and can be used by poets for effects. The use of near rhyme can be accidental or an inexact substitute for perfect rhyme used by a poet who can't think of one, or it can be intentional, used because the poet wanted that effect. It doesn't necessarily indicate a failure to find a perfect rhyme. Widely used types of near rhyme include:
  - **Assonance,** in which only the vowel sound in the stressed syllable of a word is repeated.
  - **Consonance,** in which only the final consonant sound is repeated.
  - **Alliteration,** in which only the initial consonant sound is repeated.

Here are examples of the main types of rhyme, taken from nursery rhymes:

RHYME TYPES	
Name	**Example**
End rhyme	Tom, Tom the piper's **son** Stole a pig and away he **run**.
Initial rhyme	**One** for my master, **One** for my dame, but **None** for the little boy who Lives in the lane.
Medial rhyme	
Internal rhyme	Up Jack **got** and home did **trot**
Close rhyme	The Owl and the Pussycat went to **sea** in a beautiful **pea**-green boat
Interlaced rhyme	There was a **little** Guinea pig, Who, being **little**, was not big,
Identical rhyme	**Polly put the kettle on,** **Polly put the kettle on,**
Perfect rhyme	If I'd as much money as I could **spend**, I never would cry, "Old chairs to **mend**!"
Near rhyme	
Assonance	I went to Taffy's house, Taffy wasn't **home**. Taffy came to my house and stole a marrow **bone**.
Consonance	Little John, Little **John**, He to town is **gone**.
Alliteration	I **saw** a **ship** a-**sailing**, A-**sailing** on the **sea**

BRAIN TICKLERS—THE ANSWERS

Set # 14, pages 104–105

Answers will vary. **Possible responses:**

1. Speech genre: graduation address; letter structure; academic style; content: changes in education in the twentieth century; audience: a graduating class in an education department at a college or university; purpose: to confirm for a new generation of teachers the importance of education in the United States.

2. Speech genre: personal letter; letter structure; colloquial style; content: a calico cat named Sheba; purpose: to inform and amuse a friend with a description of Sheba.

3. Speech genre: diary entry; letter structure; colloquial style; contents: events of the day; purpose: to relieve tension by committing the disconcerting events of the day to paper.

4. Speech genre: official government proclamation (specifically, this is the Emancipation Proclamation); proclamation structure; government style; content: freeing the slaves; purpose: to inform the country and world of the executive act by which the slaves have been freed and to persuade all who might think to defy the proclamation that they do so at the risk of military action from the government of the United States in support of the freedom of any former slave.

5. Speech genre: joke; dialogue structure; colloquial style; content: nonsense repetitions until the end when there is a surprising "sense"; purpose: to trick the other person into saying "I am a monkey."

Set # 15, page 110

HEADS IN CHAPTER TWO

Chapter Title
- CHAPTER TWO "Confer, Converse, and Otherwise Hobnob": Informal Talk with Others
- *CHAPTER TWO* is in a fancy font, all caps, centered and red. The title is also centered, red, and in the same font, but larger—with important words having initial caps.

Subhead
- HOW DOES COMMUNICATION HAPPEN?
- THE ART OF CONVERSATION
- Thick sans serif font, all caps, centered, and red, but smaller than the chapter title.

Sub-Subhead 1
- A moment of understanding
- Finding a unit of communication
- Defining an utterance
- Response to an utterance
- Looking from the same perspective
- Orality vs. literacy
- Understanding the communication circle
- Avoiding communication problems
- Talking about feelings
- Types of conversation
- How to have good face-to-face conversations
- Phone conversations and their etiquette
- E-mail and postal letter conversations and their etiquette
- Instant messaging and its etiquette
- SMS text messaging and its etiquette
- Tweets and direct messages and their etiquette
- Videochats and their etiquette
- Audiochats and their etiquette
- Hints for choosing conversation media
- In Futura (a plain, sans serif font), with the first letter larger and being the only one capped. Flush left, red, and smaller than the subheads.

HEADS IN CHAPTER TWO, cont.

Sub-Subhead 2
- Preventing misunderstandings
- Limitations of the "Moment of Understanding" diagram
- A link in the chain
- Finalization
- Presuppositions
- It all depends on your point of view: Deixis
- Levels of engagement
- Getting to know you
- After the opener
- After the introductions
- Etiquette in face-to-face conversation
- In Futura (a plain, sans serif font), with important words capped. Flush left, red, and smaller than sub-subhead one.

Set # 16, pages 114–117

1. a. iii. **Possible response**: The ellipsis points show a semantic pause—I think she's really angry, and the exclamation point shows her emphasis through the polite word, *please*.

    b. iii. Since there are multiple aunts, there must not be a comma before *Susie*; since there is only one uncle, there may or may not be a comma before *Henry*. The material in quotation marks should be limited to the word *Huck*. The choice between dashes and parentheses is hard to make— one might argue for either. The exclamation point or lack of it could also be argued.

2. a. **Possible response**: Paine uses typography—both capitalization and italics—to indicate specific words to stress. His long sentences are well thought out and logically organized, and the structure is clearly indicated by his use of punctuation, which is a good guide to pauses. His parenthetical remarks delineated by commas ("in this crisis," "like

hell,") I would signal by a change of pitch. I would read a couple of places differently than he has indicated: I would read as if substituting a colon for the comma after "yet we have this consolation with us," and as if deleting the parentheses around "*not only to* TAX." The only place I see orthography mattering is for " 'Tis" instead of "It is," so I would be careful to read it as written.

b. Paying attention to Poe's orthography called my attention to certain spellings that are now considered British English (*cheque, labour*) and certain words of foreign origin: *Monsieur, Dupin, meerschaum, francs*, and *escritoire*. I also noticed the use of "eh" as a sound to indicate a tag question, and the "puff" sound Dupin makes as he smokes his pipe. The use of the initial with a long dash to conceal the name of the person who is too important to have his (fictional) identity revealed, is a clever touch. Poe does not use typography to inform me about how to read the excerpt, but he uses commas and dashes extravagantly in the first half. I would contrast D's drawling, pause-marked teasing of G—— with the long sentences in the final paragraph, particularly the final, multi-predicate sentence that shows the prefect tumbling over himself to leave the house.

Set # 17, pages 122–123

Possible response:

Typography: Franklin uses italics and capitalization to call attention to words that require stress.

Orthography: Franklin uses an apostrophe to show the pronunciation of the past participles *bak'd, purchas'd, conquer'd*, and *nurtur'd* without the *-ed* being pronounced as a separate syllable. I gather from this that at one time the *-ed* was pronounced. The only other use I noted was *Tho'* spelled without the final *ugh*, which does nothing for the pronunciation anyway. I noticed that *expence* was not spelled with an *s* and *favour* was spelled with a *u*, both of which I put down to British spelling.

Punctuation: I would substitute a colon for the comma after "upon this" in the first sentence and after "no more Use" in the last sentence of III. I also find some extra commas that suggest what seem to me to be unnecessary pauses, for example after "consider" in the first sentence of I.

Figurative Language: Franklin, himself, calls attention to his simile, comparing an Empire to a cake. "Mother Country" is a personification, as is "Friends of Liberty."

Idioms: "rising of Mobs" and "uses his Wife ill"

Irony: The tone of the whole is ironic. Franklin is describing in detail the British attitude and actions toward their American colonies but couching it as advice on how to destroy an empire, which is—needless to say—not the British Empire's intention.

Other Patterns: consonance in "Ships and Seamen" and "Bullets and Bayonets"

Set # 18, pages 129–130

Answers will vary. **Possible responses:**

1. The turnips were not *on the table*, but *in the bathtub*.

2. The turnips were not *stacked* on the table, but *piled* in the bathtub.

3. The turnips were both *piled in the bathtub* and *stashed in the linen cupboard*.

4. The chickens were neither *white* nor *brown*.

5. The chickens were *neither* white nor brown, but a delicate shade of *lavender*.

6. "In the progress of *politics*, as in the common occurrences of *life*, we are not only apt to *forget* the ground we have traveled over, but frequently neglect to *gather up experience* as we go." *The Crisis* Number III, Thomas Paine

7. "Those who expect to *reap the blessings* of freedom, must, like men, *undergo the fatigues* of supporting it." *The Crisis* Number IV, Thomas Paine

8. "There is a dignity in the *warm passions of a whig*, which is never to be found in the *cold malice of a tory*." *The Crisis* Number VI, Thomas Paine

9. "It is not a little remarkable that in every case reported by ancient history in which government has been established with deliberation and consent, the task of framing it has not been committed to an *assembly* of men, but has been performed by some *individual citizen* of preeminent wisdom and approved integrity." *Federalist Paper No. 38*, Madison

10. I didn't say to meet at the *green house*: I said, "Meet me at the *greenhouse!*"

Set # 19, page 146

Answers will vary. See Appendix C, page 261, for an example.

Set # 20, page 148

Answers will vary. See Appendix C, page 265, for an example.

Set # 21, page 151

Answers will vary. See Appendix C, page 268, for an example.

CHAPTER FOUR

Composing a Speech

"It's a flat failure," said the speaker of his short speech. "The ceremony was rendered ludicrous by the speaker's poor presentation," commented the correspondent from the London *Times*. "Anyone more dull and commonplace it would not be easy to produce." And yet, the hour and fifty-seven minute featured address on that occasion by Edward Everett, former governor of Massachusetts, is long forgotten. And the failure? Why, you know it yourself! It's the Gettysburg Address, and President Lincoln was reportedly still fiddling with his 269 words while he waited to speak.

Since a good rate for platform speaking is 125 words per minute, we can estimate that President Lincoln spoke for about two minutes. This is, in fact, confirmed by Edward Everett's comment on the president's remarks in a letter he sent to Lincoln later: "I should be glad if I could flatter myself that I came as near to the central idea of the occasion, in two hours, as you did in two minutes." And this brings us to the key point of this chapter—no matter for what occasion you are preparing to speak, no matter for how brief or how long a period of time, no matter for what audience or on which subject, no matter in what style or using which particular speech genre—the goal of your preparation is to give you the scaffolding so that you can deliver an utterance. This point is so important that we're going to review what it means. One way to say it is that you should judge your communication by whether it is finalized (that is, answerable), and whether it completes your desire to communicate about the given subject in the given context at the given time for the particular audience for which it is made (see pages 57–58 for more information). This means you must always be thinking of the "communication circle" (page 65) as you prepare and think of your listeners, not as passive recipients of your words, but as the next speakers in an ongoing conversation.

Note: The vocabulary used to describe different kinds of speeches can be very confusing. This is partly because the word *extemporaneous* can either mean a speech for which you get to prepare or exactly the opposite: a speech that you give on the spot, impromptu, with little or no preparation time. In debate or speech clubs, different categories and names may be used:

- *fully-prepared speeches*;
- speeches with a moderate amount of preparation (*extemporaneous speeches*);
- and speeches with only the briefest time between learning the topic and having to speak to it (*impromptu speeches*).

We're going to discuss only two types of speeches: prepared speeches and unrehearsed or impromptu speeches. In this chapter, you will learn detailed steps for the process of starting from the idea stage and developing a fully prepared speech.

SPEECH GENRE SELECTION

You may be looking at this chapter in response to a very specific assignment, such as a humorous speech titled "My First Time Behind the Wheel," a presentation called "How to Dribble and Shoot a Basketball," or an oral report on "Airport Security After 9/11." If you're working with a specific assignment, you probably already have a fairly clear idea of your speech genre (and of the content, style, and structure you'll be working with), as well as the audience, purpose, and context of your speech. If this is the case, you may want to jump ahead to Identifying Tasks and Choosing Graphic Organizers on page 178.

Now, I'm supposing if you're still with me on this page that you have a more general assignment for which you need to make decisions yourself, or that you're on your own time (not taking a course) and thinking about preparing a talk of some sort. There are many different angles from which to start your brainstorming process, and we'll explore several. Because purpose is so closely tied to the other elements of an utterance (people don't usually say to themselves, "I want to cheer someone up. Whom should it be?"), it is probably a good idea to start your brainstorming process elsewhere. So we'll look at starting with audience, subject, and speech genre.

Starting with your audience

If you have an identified audience—perhaps classmates at school or a workgroup at your jobsite—you can start by copying and filling in the body of the audience identification chart that follows (leave speech genre, structure, content, purpose, style, and context blank for now). You can download a digital copy of the *Painless Speaking* website.

Because speech genres each carry a range of audiences, as soon as you have identified an audience, you have some idea of appropriate speech genres and appropriate subjects. You will probably not prepare an epic poem or a formal rebuttal for three-year-olds, nor are you likely to speak to them about the effects of Dutch elm disease on the profile of American town centers or the need to rethink the solid waste plan in your county. In most cases, ideas about your audience will guide your decisions in a positive way. If you're speaking to your class for example, unless you're going to create a pretend scenario, you can probably sort through the list of speech genres on page 95 and select the ones that fit your audience pretty quickly.

If you will be speaking to people you know well, you may not even have to give the subject much thought—you may already have a good sense of the interests that you and your audience share, and what you can talk about that will get and hold their attention. Perhaps they'd even be willing to hear about a topic they're not (yet) especially interested in, just because *you* are speaking about it!

If you will be speaking to an audience you don't know well, a good place to start is with anything audience members have in common. This could be their age, the place they live, their ethnic background, the fact that they all know you, their choice to take a speech class, or an appreciation of stand-up comedy, pickles, or Russian folk art. If you simply do not have enough information, then it's a good idea to make your topic something you are passion-ate about; your enthusiasm and knowledge of your subject is your best chance for spurring interest when you have no other leads.

Finding an authentic purpose for a particular audience is essential. Even if your speech is "just an exercise" for a class, creating an utterance depends on having a response in mind. The more clarity you can bring to this key element of the relationship between you and your audience, the better guidance you will have for evaluating how to create the framework for your speech.

AUDIENCE IDENTIFICATION CHART

Name:_____ Date:_____

Speech genre:_____ Structure:_____

Content:_____

Purpose (desired response):_____

Style:_____ Context:_____

AUDIENCE IDENTIFICATION

Who is your audience? (Write a detailed description.)

1. Describe the age range of your audience.

2. Is your audience hostile or friendly?

3. What can you expect that your audience already knows about the content of your speech?

4. How many people make up the audience?

5. Is your audience known to you or not? If known, in what capacity?

6. What is your audience's cultural/ethnic background?

7. In some ways, your audience may be like you. In some ways, your audience may not resemble you at all. Use this chart to help you think about how your audience is similar to and different from you. Then explain your answers.

Characteristic	The same as you	Different from you
attitudes	_____	_____
beliefs	_____	_____
values	_____	_____
interests	_____	_____
prior knowledge	_____	_____
experience	_____	_____
political views	_____	_____
socioeconomic status	_____	_____

Which of the factors may be important, given the content and purpose of your speech? Circle the factors that will shape how you prepare to speak to your chosen audience. Then write some observations about each one.

Attitudes

Beliefs

Values

Interests

Prior knowledge

Experience

Political views

Socioeconomic status

Do you want your brother to feel that lending you his mountain bike was the finest decision he ever made? Do you want a two-year-old to commit to keeping his shoes on in the park? Do you want all your classmates to sign a petition requesting that the school buy a set of timpani for the orchestra? In each of the utterances mentioned, you might inform, persuade, express your feelings and/or thoughts, and entertain in order to achieve your purpose.

GENEROUS BROTHER	
Inform	Guess what! I won the bike race!
Express	I'm so glad that you were generous enough to let me borrow your bike. You're really a great brother!
Entertain	You should have seen the leader when I passed him! He had this look on his face like, "Where'd she come from?!"
Persuade	Not only that, I beat my best time on my old bike by 14 seconds racing on yours. Your bike is just tops, and I wouldn't have won without it. I hope you'll let me use it again when we have a rematch!

PERCUSSION-DEPRIVED CLASSMATES	
Inform	To play lots of orchestra music authentically, we need to have the drums known as timpani at our school.
Persuade	The orchestra without timpani would be like our jazz band sans its drum set. We wouldn't even think of that as a possibility. Why would we do to our orchestra what we wouldn't do to our jazz band?
Express	This means a lot to me as a percussionist—when I have to stand empty-handed and watch the rest of the orchestra play an incomplete piece, I feel sad and deprived, not just on my own behalf, but on the whole school community's behalf
Entertain	And you better believe that if we make the effort and raise the funds for these timpani, *I* get to be the first one to play them. And you better believe there's nowhere you can go in this school where you won't know that the timpani have arrived!

SHOELESS TWO-YEAR-OLD	
Inform	Now we're going to go to the park.
Express	I would be really happy if you could keep your shoes on today at the park.
Persuade	If you can keep your shoes on the whole time we're at the park, then you can go barefoot once we get back to your house.
Entertain	"Hi, Ben. I'm Mr. Shoe. Please don't take me off! I might get lost. Then I would be sad. Boo hoo hoo!"

Starting with the content

Let's say that you already have a subject in mind. Perhaps you want to speak about your pet skunk. Or maybe you are planning to give some kind of response to reading or viewing *Romeo and Juliet*. If you start with a subject—no matter what kind—it will help shape your thinking about your purpose, audience, and speech genre. In fact, your subject may have shaped one or more of these elements already.

What kind of purpose might you have for writing about your pet skunk? This topic is open to a wide variety of purposes. Maybe you want to persuade others that skunks make wonderful pets, or you may want to share a funny story about what your skunk did to lessen the irrational bias you've observed against skunks. Perhaps you want to inform people about aspects of skunk life they probably know nothing about, or use skunks as an example to teach people about words that they use everyday that come from American Indian languages (*skunk* comes from the Algonquian language, as does *raccoon*) to underscore the influence of Native American culture.

Like the subject of skunks, there are many subjects that you can speak about with a wide variety of purposes. Your choice of purpose will be shaped by the audience and speech genre. Narrowed subjects, or subject matter stated as questions, are often more closely tied to a particular purpose. *Athletic scholarships* is a fairly open subject. *How important are athletic scholarships?* requires evaluative thinking and suggests an audience who might receive athletic scholarships, donate to them, or be in some other way influenced by their existence, as well as a purpose of getting the audience to think or commit to some attitude about athletic scholarships.

Starting with a speech genre

Different speech classes and clubs have different names for different categories of speeches. Here are the names of kinds of speeches using vocabulary employed in some speech classes and clubs and the speech genres that match. If you're not in a speech class, just look at the right-hand column to get some ideas—most people either have a couple of favorite speech genres, or can find one they'd like to try out. You can also refer to the speech genre list on page 95.

MATCHING SPEECH CATEGORIES TO SPEECH GENRES	
Category	**Speech Genres**
Speech to inform	biography demonstration directions history how-to proposal research report
Speech to persuade (convince, give opinion)	argument case study commentary editorial manifesto political platform response/rebuttal review (book, movie, concert, etc.)
Speech to entertain	anecdote joke poem roast story
Speech from personal experience	anecdote autobiography demonstration how-to monologue slide show
Speech to stimulate or arouse an audience	address dedication eulogy invocation prayer promotion rally speech

SUBJECT DEVELOPMENT

However you begin the process, sooner or later you need to choose a subject for your speech. The following three brainstorming methods—using fields of knowledge, brainstorming with words, and brainstorming with images—can help give you ideas.

| FINDING SUBJECTS FROM FIELDS OF KNOWLEDGE ||
Field of Knowledge	Categories
Literature	• types of • authors • movements • of different cultures • history of • individual works
Technology	• types of • inventors • effects on society • of different cultures • history of • individual works
Science	• fields of • scientists • professions in • current challenges • history of • discoveries or research
History	• of places • of people • of wars • of countries • political
Government	• forms of • politicians • history of • examples of • relationships between and among • spying
Athletics	• types of • competitions • athletes • history • teams • scholarships
Society	• etiquette • theatre • communication • television • entertainment • movies • music • psychology

Going through a random collection of topics all jumbled together can sometimes get you thinking about a topic you'd like to use for your speech. Try this list or the visual form on the next page.

airplanes	construction	inventions
rockets	graphic design	magic
pyramids	jewelry	castles
painter	cars	Holocaust
plumbing	recreation	trains
holidays	technology	folklore
mountains	black hole	apartheid
Shakespeare	dynamite	your favorite book
spirituality	honor	musicals
Albania	gardens	pets
cuisine	crocodiles	libraries
mysteries	costumes	crafts
reality television	astrology	electric eels
pioneers	Hawaii	photography
dragons	zoos	architecture
pickling	tsars	glory
explorers	soccer	waterfalls
cartoons	rodents	seeing-eye dogs
ethics	fireworks	cancer
stars	dinosaurs	Mississippi River
pigs	gems	cartography
justice	alphabets	democracy
myths	rabbits	Loch Ness Monster
crafts	graphic novels	Babylon
tools	Olympics	the brain
hats	fishing	paleontology
Egypt	computers	radio
business	perfume	orienteering
oceans	farms	transportation
infancy	pests	color
robots	communication	chemistry
ballet	movies	mountains

BRAIN TICKLERS
Set # 22

1. Either starting from an assignment or using your own starting point, come up with a subject, audience, purpose, and speech genre for your speech.
2. Download the audience identification chart from the *Painless Speaking* website and fill in as much as you can at this point.

(Answers are on page 203.)

Narrowing your subject using questions

Because the process of listening is so complex, 125 words per minute is *the* comfortable speed for platform speeches. So you need to narrow your subject enough that you can speak a finalized utterance in the allotted time. A narrowed subject also helps keep your research manageable. But how much to narrow your subject to fit your speaking time is not an exact science. There is no way to tell you—for any possible subject you might come up with—how much you have to narrow it to fit in the speech occasion, both because there are too many possible subjects and because it partly depends on your speech genre and personal style. Remember, it's better to have a bit more information than you actually need or use in your speech than it is to have too little information to complete the speech you're expected to or want to make, so if you're not sure, go a little broader than you think you'll need.

When we narrow a subject, we can look at it in one of two ways—as a *thing in itself* or as a *thing in a context*. In the first case, we analyze its attributes, the defining characteristics that make it what it is. In the second case, we analyze its relationships to something outside itself. The charts on the following pages show how this works. Note that not every question in the chart will work for every subject, but you may be able to change the wording a bit and make it work.

NARROWING A SUBJECT: THE DEFINITIVE GUIDE

Attributes—The Subject as a Thing in Itself

Type of Analysis	Questions
operational	How do you do it? What is the story of it? How does it work? How does/did it happen? How is/was it made? What does it require for its operation?
structural	What are its parts? What variations occur in it? What is it made of? What systems form it? What examples are there of it?
sensory	What is the experience of it like? How does it move? How does it look? What textures and weight does it have? How does it sound and under what conditions? How does it taste? How does it smell?

CONTEXT—THE SUBJECT IN RELATIONSHIP

Type of Analysis	Questions
theoretical	How does it demonstrate the theory of __? How does it manifest the outlook/perspective of __?
classification	What categories does it fit into? Under which systems can it be classified?
situational	Where is it? Under what circumstances does it exist or come into existence? Why does it occur/happen when and where it does?
relational	What kind of interactions take place between it and __? What relationships exist between it and __?
thematic	What is associated with it in people's minds? What are its major meaning strands?

CONTEXT—THE SUBJECT IN RELATIONSHIP, cont.	
Type of Analysis	**Questions**
meaning	What does it mean (and to whom)? How can it be interpreted? Why was it made?
cause-and-effect	What are its causes? What are its effects? What events lead or led up to it? What events result(ed) from it (and other causal factors)?
historical	What other events happened along with it? What events preceded and followed it? What relationship does it have with past, concurrent, and future events?
utilization	What is its purpose? What are its current or historical uses? What could it be used for?
response	What actions, feelings, and beliefs arise in response to it? How does it change the way people think, feel, and act?
problem/solution	Can it be solved and, if so, how? How can it be limited or mitigated? What can be done to change or eliminate it? How can it be applied in a new context?
comparative	What is it like, and how? How does it differ from other similar things? What is an analogy/metaphor for it or some aspect of it?
logical	Why is it valid? How can it be justified? What reasons and examples support it?
emotional	How do people (I) feel about it and why? What could change people's feelings about it? What will people do as a result of how they feel about it?
evaluative	What is its value? How well does it __? How important is it in relation to __? From what perspective(s) does it (not) have value?

As you consider how to narrow your subject, you can use these four criteria to help you:

1. Is the narrowed subject you're considering appropriate to you and your audience, purpose, and context? Make sure it's not too technical, ordinary, or trivial.
2. Do you have access to sufficient material to research your narrowed subject idea?
3. Do you feel sure you can create a finalized utterance with this narrowed topic in the time allotted?
4. Given your current knowledge of the narrowed subject, will you have enough time to research and prepare your speech?

BRAIN TICKLERS
Set # 23

Use the question approach or some other approach that you find useful to narrow your subject.

(Answers are on page 203.)

Identifying tasks and choosing graphic organizers

After you identify a question to help you narrow your subject, you can use the following chart to identify a task that will form the basis (though probably not the entire matter) of your speech and a graphic organizer to help you structure your research and your speech. The first column shows the types of analysis from the previous chart. The second column restates one or more questions from that analysis as a relationship. The third column names the tasks and identifies the graphic organizer that is most apt.

Remember that a speech genre is hardly ever composed entirely of a single task; a task is often better used to describe a single passage or paragraph. Use the graphic organizer *only as it serves your purposes*, and use multiple graphic organizers, if necessary. You can download the graphic organizers from the *Painless Speaking* website at *http://www.edreinvented.com/products/painless-speaking/* and find them in Appendix A.

ANALYSIS, RELATIONSHIP, TASKS, AND GRAPHIC ORGANIZERS		
Type of Analysis	**Relationship**	**Task and Graphic Organizer**
Comparative	differences or opposition	Compare/Contrast Type 1
Comparative	similarities	Compare/Contrast Type 2
Operational	change over time	Define/Describe Type 1
Operational	functioning	Define/Describe Type 2
Structural	components/examples	Define/Describe Type 3
Sensory	attributes/description	Define/Describe Type 4
Relational	associations	Define/Describe Type 5
Theoretical, Meaning, Thematic	meaning	Define/Describe Type 6
Utilization	purpose	Define/Describe Type 7
Evaluative	value/criteria for judging	Define/Describe Type 8
Situational	environment	Define/Describe Type 9
Any		List
Logical	hypothesis	Argue Type 1
	proposition/support or statement/proof	Argue Type 2
	question/answer	Argue Type 3
Problem/Solution	problem/solution resolution	Argue Type 4
Cause-and-Effect Response Emotional	causal chain	Narrate/Sequence Type 1
Historical	order of events in time	Narrate/Sequence Type 2
Classification	hierarchy	Classify/Categorize Type 1

BRAIN TICKLERS
Set # 24

Using the preceding chart and the graphic organizers in Appendix A (pages 239–251), identify one or more graphic organizers that may be of use to you in researching and structuring your paper.

(Answers are on page 203.)

RESEARCH AND SOURCES

Researching is a unique set of activities that fit with your particular speech. Different subjects or the same subject handled in different ways could take you to entirely different sources. If you are planning to speak about a personal experience, your research may consist of consulting your own memory, or perhaps a journal or a close friend. Research could also mean hours on the Internet or in the library.

Consider whether these types of references—recent or historical—will be useful for your speech.

TYPES OF REFERENCES	
Almanac	Gazetteer
Atlas	Guidebook
Bibliography	Handbook
Biographical Dictionary	Index
Brochure	Newspaper
Chronologies	Periodical
Concordance	Quotation Dictionary
Dictionary of Language	Textbooks
Directory	Thesaurus
Encyclopedia	Yearbook

For Internet research, these sites have collections of sources and may be particularly helpful in figuring out which individual sources will serve your needs.

DIGITAL REFERENCE COLLECTIONS	
Source type	**Internet Location**
all types of references	*http://refdesk.com*
dictionaries	*http://onelook.com*
encyclopedias	*http://www.encyclopedia.com*
newspapers	*http://onlinenewspapers.com*
quotations	*http://www.bartleby.com/quotations/*

The CIA World Factbook is another good source to know about for up-to-date information about countries around the world, as well as some historic data: *https://www.cia.gov/library/publications/the-world-factbook/*

Choosing good sources is important. If you are doing research in print or digital sources, the particular sources you choose will also be guided by the precise demands of your speech. If you need up-to-date information, you'll seek out current copyrights, while historical research may take you on a hunt for books that are older or even out of print. For example, if you were researching slang in the 1960s, you might wish to find original documents that demonstrate the usages, and that would lead you to sources that are more than 50 years old. You might also want to find the latest research that reviews slang in the 1960s, in which case you'd want recent publications.

Although you usually will seek out sources that are unbiased and authoritative, a speech about public opinion or people's response to a particular event might lead you to actually look for bias and illogical comments, perhaps using sources like Twitter and other social networking sites. You might also need less reliable sources if part of your speech will involve rebutting their opinions.

It's not always easy to evaluate writers and thinkers in a field with which you're not familiar. Their credentials, a sense that they have mastery of the material, and a sense of integrity and intellectual honesty are signs to look for. On the other hand, someone who glosses over problems or fails to address key opposition points may not provide trustworthy information in other respects. Your reference librarian can provide assistance in this and other cases.

Here are some tips for researching on the Internet.

1. Use a good search engine for your purposes.
   - Bing is designed for shopping research.
   - Wolfram Alpha is a knowledge base.
   - Google has just about everything.

   Choosing wisely will help ensure you get apt results.

2. Try using the search engine descriptions to separate out the valuable results and only go to sites that look promising.
   - Skim material for relevance.
   - Print the material to document your search (and if you have limited time online), making sure to get the full URL so you can properly document the source and return to the same location.

3. If the information you need on a page won't print (either because you've got white text on a darker background or because it's programmed not to), sometimes you can copy and paste it into a document and print it from there. As recommended in 2, be sure to obtain the URL.

Now that you've got your sources, what next? Read! Highlight or take notes (or both) as you read, and just become familiar with the subject so that you can take the next step: Take a shot at answering your question. Remember your question? If you've chosen your sources well, you've now got enough background and factual support to start building an answer, and this answer is the **thesis** of your speech. So, depending on which question you were focusing on, your thesis might turn out something like one of these:

Architecture plays a symbolic role in the *Fellowship of the Rings* movie.

The meaning of "Let's roll" became fixed forever as a patriotic cry of the free citizen defending his country on September 11, 2001.

Analysis of the shopping scene in B____ reveals how organic and vegetarian food availability has influenced the buying habits of self-identified meat-and-potatoes consumers.

After you have identified your thesis, it is time to begin taking notes on the material you need to support your thesis.

When taking notes on research materials, many people find it easiest to note each bit of information on a separate index card, on which is indicated the source of the information. (You need the source information both in case you want to return to the original source for some reason and in order to credit the information, if necessary, in your speech, so record the details, including page numbers, carefully.) This system allows you to shuffle the cards into various orders to try different organizations for your speech. A heading on each note card will help when it's time to group them.

Architecture and lighting—general comment

Lord of the Rings: The Fellowship of the Ring reviewed by Charity Bishop
http://www.charitysplace.com/review/review-fellowship.htm

"The architecture and construction of the many sets, ranging from the dark and foreboding Orthanc (where the evil wizard dwells) to the brightly-lit Elfin city of Rivendell are nothing less than magical. Lighting creates a mood; the places inhabited by good are often bright and cheering, or subtly blue in the darkness; places dominated by evil are dark and foreboding, grotesque, chilling."

COMPOSING YOUR SPEECH

The president is about to deliver a speech, and you know he's got every single carefully chosen word in front of him on the teleprompter. So maybe you think that's what preparing a speech is—getting everything in order so that you can *read* your speech. Well, that is, in fact, what some people do. And, let's face it, when national security and world peace are on the agenda, saying things "just so" is absolutely crucial.

But some people feel gypped by speakers who read their words. They want the sense of presence and involvement that comes from two people who meet in conversation and are not only meeting face-to-face but also making eye contact. That's why the president uses a teleprompter instead of a written copy of the speech and works really hard to look natural and conversational when, actually, every word, every intonation, is carefully crafted. You might think that memorizing your speech is a possible answer. But there are problems with that approach, too. When you actually meet your audience, if you've misjudged them or the context at all, your pre-speech decisions will make it evident that you're here-and-now talk is actually prefabricated. And—what if you lose your place, forget your lines, blank on what comes next? There's a better way, say the speech experts.

First of all, it's probably a pretty good shot that whatever subject you're trying to master and share, it's at least a *little* less crucial than the fate of the nation as told by the commander in chief. Second, there's a middle way between memorizing your speech and reading it word for word. Speaking from notes—either an outline, your graphic organizer, or a large note card (or several small ones if you prefer)—can give you the best of both worlds, plus an added advantage that neither of the other methods has.

WHY SPEAK FROM NOTES WITHOUT MEMORIZING?

1	**Like reading,** speaking from notes allows you to have material that you must speak verbatim for accuracy (e.g., quotations) right at your fingertips.
2	**Like memorizing,** speaking from notes allows you to make eye contact with your audience because you're free to look away from the material when you're comfortable doing so.
3	**Additionally,** speaking from notes encourages you to speak from your knowledge of the material, rather than from the knowledge of a particular set of words about that material. This allows you the freedom to adapt your speech to the events, insights, and reactions you receive as you speak.

BRAIN TICKLERS
Set # 25

1. If your subject requires it, do appropriate research to find material for your speech. Read through your material and identify a thesis statement that answers your question. Write your thesis statement.
2. Take notes to support the speech you will give on your thesis.

(Answers are on page 203.)

Supporting your thesis

To prove or support your thesis, you must back it up with some of the information you garnered from your research. Ten kinds of support for your thesis include:

1. Statistics
2. Specific facts
3. Interview material
4. Studies
5. Surveys
6. Quotation of authority opinion
7. Examples
8. Anecdotal evidence
9. Audience activity such as a survey, demonstration, or quiz
10. Trends

You should arrange your support in some logical order, choosing one of the basic organizing patterns that are used in speechcraft (but note that the list is not exhaustive).

COMMON ORGANIZING PATTERNS	
Compare/Contrast	by category or feature
Define/Describe	by spatial arrangement or by system or feature
List	specific to general general to specific
Argue	increasing or decreasing importance
Narrate/Sequence	step-by-step chronological
Classify/Categorize	by features of the class or category

BRAIN TICKLERS
Set # 26

Choose an organizing pattern and arrange your notes in the order you have decided upon.

(Answers are on page 203.)

Filling in your graphic organizer(s) and outlining

Filling in your graphic organizer(s) and outlining are two means to the same end: finding and organizing the key points that support your thesis in a form from which you can speak. Opinion is divided on whether you should use complete sentences (sentence outline) or phrases (topic outline), so experiment to see what works best for you. Here are the rules for how to construct an outline:

1. Use the headings on your note cards to group related ideas together.
2. Identify the main points that support your thesis. Each main point becomes a main topic in your outline and is identified by a Roman numeral followed by a period.
3. Subtopics of diminishing importance are indented and identified with (in this order) capital letters, Arabic numerals, small letters, Arabic numerals in parentheses, and small letters in parentheses. There must be a minimum of two subtopics to support the preceding topic. With the exception of numerals and small letters in parentheses, each subtopic identifier is followed by a period.
4. Capitalize the first word of each topic. In a sentence outline, end with a period. In a topic outline, do not use end punctuation.
5. Usually, topics of the same importance are parallel in construction. This means that they have the same grammatical form, for example all full sentences, all starting with a verb ending in -*ing*; etc.
6. Usually, no less than three main points are necessary to support a thesis.

NOTE

Some speech teachers have students create separate outlines for the introduction, body, and conclusion of their speech so that they can clearly see these important structural divisions. If you outline this way, you may not need to have more than one main point in your introduction or conclusion. Feel free to choose either form unless you are preparing for a class or club and have been instructed to follow a particular approach.

Models of Outline Form

TITLE

I.
   A.
      1.
      2.
II.
   A.
      1.
      2.
         a.
         b.
            (1)
            (2)
               (a)
               (b)
   B.
III.
   A.
   B.
   C.
IV.
   A.
      1.
      2.
   B.
V.
   A.
   B.

TITLE
INTRODUCTION
I.
   A.
      1.
      2.
BODY
I.
   A.
      1.
      2.
         a.
         b.
            (1)
            (2)
               (a)
               (b)
   B.
II.
   A.
   B.
   C.
III.
   A.
      1.
      2.
   B.
CONCLUSION
I.
   A.
   B.

Here is an outline of part of this chapter for demonstration purposes. You may compare it to the actual text.

COMPOSING A SPEECH

  I. SPEECH GENRE SELECTION
    A. Starting with your audience
    B. Starting with the content
    C. Starting with a speech genre
  II. SUBJECT DEVELOPMENT
    A. Narrowing your subject using questions
    B. Identifying tasks and choosing graphic organizers
  III. RESEARCH AND SOURCES
  IV. COMPOSING YOUR SPEECH
    A. Supporting your thesis
    B. Filling in your graphic organizer(s) and outlining

Notice that the outline points have, in this case, translated into the headings in the text. But I have to tell you, this is *not* the outline that I started with. As I developed the chapter, the outline changed. This will also likely happen to you, so be prepared, and consider making your outline in pencil. You can see the parallel construction by looking at the first word of each of the subtopics. You can also see that I chose to use a topic outline, rather than a sentence outline.

BRAIN TICKLERS
Set # 27

Construct an outline for your speech. For right now, you can leave out the introduction and conclusion—they require special attention, and we'll focus on them in a bit. Just get the body of your speech organized.

(Answers are on page 203.)

Looking for tasks

At some point, you need to decide whether you will speak from your outline or graphic organizer. Since many people speak from outlines, I'm going to use that as a reference, but if you prefer to use the graphic organizer, just substitute that in your mind.

The next step is to check your outline to identify any portions that can be fairly clearly identified as fitting into the six task categories: compare/contrast, define/describe, list, argue, narrate/sequence, classify/categorize. After you identify the task, refer to the chart on pages 126–127 to identify words that can have a key function in helping the listener construct a meaningful understanding of what you're saying. Using a colored pencil or marker, write these key words and phrases in appropriate places between points on your outline to show the logical relationships.

The composition process

Now that you're done with the body part of your outline, you can start composing your speech. Notice, I didn't say start *writing* your speech. There's a good reason for that. If you sit down and write your speech, unless you're an extraordinarily gifted writer, you're going to end up with a major clash of orality and literacy. All the conventions you've been taught for writing are just for that—for writing. But now, you're trying to put together something to speak, not something that has to meet the standards for written prose. Remember the things we said about the differences between orality and literacy (pages 63–64) and about the conventions in prose (like emoticons) that substitute (poorly) for the elements of paralanguage that aren't captured on paper (pages 80–82)?

- Written sentences can be more complex than spoken sentences, and readers have more time to think and review than listeners.
- Written sentences are not planned to be interactive, so writers try to anticipate readers' responses and incorporate them.
- Readers can process more information than listeners.
- Listeners have less recall than readers.

So here's what you can do: you can make up your speech out loud and *then* write it down. Oh, you might refine the language in your writing, make it a little more literary. But by *starting* with oral language, you can make sure that you're attuned to the needs of your audience.

BRAIN TICKLERS
Set # 28

With your outline in hand, stand up, and start talking. Having a timer handy will help you make a judgment about how long the material will be once you add your introduction and conclusion. Do this three times. Make notes after each trial. It's okay if you say different words each time. It's also okay if some words start to gel and remain the same each time.

(Answers are on page 203.)

REFINING YOUR SPEECH

Now that you've said words out loud, you can really say you've got the beginnings of a speech. Next, you need to check your logic and language, add an introduction and conclusion, and come up with one or more visual aids, if appropriate.

Logic and logical fallacies

A **logical fallacy** is a faulty argument in which something besides reason contributes to the conclusion drawn. Many fallacies have been named and categorized to make them easier to recognize and remember.

Two basic forms of reasoning are deduction and induction.

Deductive reasoning moves from the general to a specific instance of the general cases being considered. If something is true in general, and an instance is really representative of that general class, then the truth will hold for the specific instance. Syllogisms are examples of deductive reasoning.

STANDARD SYLLOGISM FORM

> Every X is Y. (All flowers are plants.)
> C is X. (A columbine is a flower.)
> Therefore, C is Y. (Therefore, a columbine is a plant.)

Fallacies in deductive reasoning come about when one of the first two statements of a syllogism is not true, for example, if C is assumed to be a member of X when it truly isn't.

Inductive reasoning moves from the particular to the general. It is harder to achieve certainty with this kind of logic because you have to determine when you've looked at enough particular examples to be able to draw a general rule that will hold good in all cases.

This is not a complete list of logical fallacies, but it includes some of the more common ones.

SOME LOGICAL FALLACIES

Insufficient Evidence

hasty generalization—drawing a conclusion with too little supporting evidence

fallacy of exclusion—leaving out evidence that would change the outcome of an inductive argument (in which one derives general laws from particular circumstances)

oversimplification—making a complex issue simple by ignoring some of its aspects

Cause-and-Effect Mistakes

gambler's due—assuming that after a certain number of events of a similar kind, things are "due" to change

post hoc, ergo propter hoc—literally "after this, therefore, on account of it"; assuming that something that comes after is caused by something that comes before

slippery slope—assuming that one thing inevitably leads to another

false analogy—assuming that because of some (superficial) resemblances, conclusions drawn from one case apply to another

Emotion Rather than Reason

appeal to hate—claiming that if people don't like an idea, it should be dismissed

appeal to force—attempting to persuade by threat or actual force

guilt by association—inferring a person's character by looking at the company s/he chooses

special pleading—presenting a case as being outside the rules (can contain a more specific appeal to emotion, such as **appeal to pity**)

BRAIN TICKLERS
Set # 29

Check your current set of notes and review the body of your speech. Is your logic valid? If not, rethink your arguments, returning if necessary to your research to find additional (or better) support for your points, or even changing your points. Redo anything that needs redoing.

(Answers are on page 203.)

Vivid language and voice

Figurative language (pages 119–120) can add punch to your words. However, if you use it, make sure that you employ devices that your audience will be able to interpret at listening speed without the benefit of "looking back." **Sensory language** engages the senses of sight, hearing, smell, taste, and touch by using images that appeal to these senses. Sensory language helps people imagine what you are speaking about

On the other hand, words like *smart, good, nice, interesting, funny, pretty, like,* and *very* are overused and don't give your audience much to work with. Substituting a synonym (a thesaurus can help) is usually an excellent idea.

Quotations can do more than just support your thesis: they can add piquant, evocative language to your speech. Because they're someone else's words and phrasing, they change the pace and style for a moment or two. If you find an apt quotation, use it. For examples of speeches that include quotations, see the speeches by Robert F. Kennedy (page 256) and Ronald Reagan (page 258) in Appendix B.

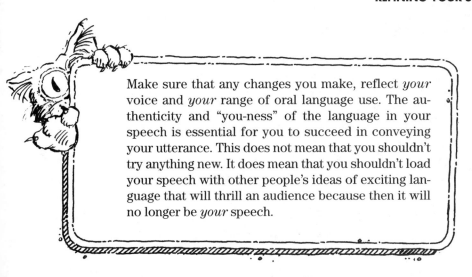

Make sure that any changes you make, reflect *your* voice and *your* range of oral language use. The authenticity and "you-ness" of the language in your speech is essential for you to succeed in conveying your utterance. This does not mean that you shouldn't try anything new. It does mean that you shouldn't load your speech with other people's ideas of exciting language that will thrill an audience because then it will no longer be *your* speech.

While we're talking about language choices, we should also discuss using exact words v. using whatever words happen to come to mind in the moment. Quotations are an example of words that need to be said exactly as written, but they are not the only ones. Exact wording is also important in these cases:

- **When you make reference to what you said earlier or to a catch phrase or keyword.** If you use a synonym rather than the exact word, your audience may not follow
- **When your words provide a cue for someone else.** A cue needs to be said exactly as written.
- **When you're using a performative verb (see page 96) in a customary way.** If you don't use the right words, the thing you meant to perform may not happen.
- **When you're telling a joke.** Often there are certain words that are key to the humor.

If there are words in your speech that must be said exactly, it's a good idea to mark your notes in some way so that you can easily locate them. It's also a good idea to choose a type size that will allow you to read the words, even in dim light.

Your introduction

At some moment, by some indication—dimming lights, an announcement, your appearance—a hush falls over the room. It is the moment that everyone has been waiting for. What happens now is up to you. What are you going to do with this moment?

The purpose of your introduction is to gain attention *for your specific utterance* and establish a connection with the audience. Therefore, your introduction must make a connection between you and your audience in some way that is pertinent to the particular context. There are many ways to arouse interest: this one must be focused to lead your audience into your speech.

Here are some tried and true approaches to arousing an audience's interest. Each is useful in particular circumstances.

- State clearly the context, occasion, and purpose of the gathering.
- Open with a story or anecdote or joke linked to the subject of the speech.
- Explain why you chose to speak on the particular subject you did, complimenting the audience on some quality that ties into the speech subject, if appropriate.
- Provide background information (about yourself or your subject) that is necessary to an understanding of what is to come.
- Refer to an incident with which the audience is familiar (for example, a local event or something that happened earlier in the day).
- Begin with a quotation that shows great insight, cites a recognized authority, or that you wish to refute.
- Set out a striking idea.
- State an arresting fact.
- Ask the audience a question.
- Give the audience something to ponder, which, as you tell them, you will return to at the end of your speech.
- Begin your story *in medias res* (in the middle of things) as the poet Horace recommended or in some exciting or tantalizing way.

Whatever method you use, make sure that the tone of your introduction is consistent with the tone of the body of your speech. You should not, for example, be sincere in one and sarcastic in the other.

BRAIN TICKLERS
Set # 30

Compose an introduction for your speech. In other words, come up with an idea, and speak it, continuing into the body of your speech until you are satisfied that it fits.

(Answers are on page 203.)

Your conclusion

Before you compose your conclusion, reread the section about the finalization of an utterance on pages 57–58. This section of your speech is extremely important because it is the transition between your utterance and your audience's response. Some speech experts suggest that your conclusion should be no more than one-eighth to one-tenth of the total length of your speech. Nevertheless, it is the last of your words that the audience will hear; and, therefore, the words they are most likely to remember. So ask yourself, "What do I most want people to remember?"

BRAIN TICKLERS
Set # 31

Look at the conclusion of every speech in Appendix B. Which, in your opinion, is the most memorable? Why?

(Answers are on page 203.)

Most written expository compositions end with a summary. This does not have to be so with a speech. You might summarize. But you also might

- reiterate the thesis of your speech in a new way, using a quotation from literature or poetry;
- add a final supporting insight or fact that you've saved;
- use an analogy to drive home your point;
- end with an anecdote that illustrates your meaning;
- call your audience to take action;
- request your audience to reconsider the point you asked them to ponder at the beginning of your speech;
- ask your audience if their answer to your initial question has changed; or
- invite your audience to ask questions or offer comments.

Your title

Your title should have the virtue of being either brief, clever, or both. It should, as succinctly as possible, let the audience know something about your thesis.

Remember these thesis statements (from pages 182–183)? Here they are matched with possible titles:

FROM THESIS TO TITLE

Thesis Statement	Possible Title
Architecture plays a symbolic role in the *Fellowship of the Rings* movie.	You Are What You Build
The meaning of "Let's roll" became fixed forever as a patriotic cry of the free citizen defending his country on September 11, 2001.	Let's Roll
Analysis of the shopping scene in B___reveals how organic and vegetarian food availability has influenced the buying habits of self-identified meat-and-potatoes consumers.	Tempeh Goes Mainstream

BRAIN TICKLERS
Set # 32

Brainstorm three titles for your speech. Choose your favorite.

(Answers are on page 203.)

Presentation aids

You are, of course, the chief presentation aid in your speech.
Your face, hands, and body will express a great deal of your
meaning. You may use gesture and even pantomime to get your
points across. But there are other ways, too, to take advantage
of the visual, as well as the aural, nature of a live presentation.
Here are some ideas.

PRESENTATION AIDS	
audio tape	chart
drawing	flip chart
graph	handout
list	overhead transparencies
photograph	prop
sample	presentation slides
video clip	

HELPFUL HINTS FOR USING PRESENTATION AIDS

These hints are useful whether your presentation aid is a poster, a set of PowerPoint slides, an MP3, a DVD, or some overhead transparencies.

1. The presentation aid is an aid, not the main event. Make sure to keep it in its place. Bring it out when it's called for and keep it out of sight at other times, so it doesn't distract your audience's attention.
2. Make the presentation aid simple and straightforward. Unless it's a handout, the audience will have limited time to interpret and absorb it.
3. If you use a graph, choose an appropriate type (pie chart, bar graph, line graph, etc.) for your data display and label it appropriately.
4. Make your presentation aid large enough to be seen by all.
5. Make sure any aids are sequenced properly and, if they're hard copies, right-side up prior to your speech.
6. Make sure all electronic equipment is functioning, and have a back-up plan in case it's not.
7. Make sure that all audio and video material is properly cued.
8. Keep words on presentation aids to a minimum—focus on the visual.
9. If your audience is looking at a handout or reading the words on a PowerPoint slide, they're not focusing on you. Give out your handouts at the end of the speech.
10. Don't put anything on a presentation aid that you will not explicitly refer to in your speech.
11. Limit the number of presentation aids so the focus stays on your words as you speak them.

Before you create a visual aid, decide whether you want it to show something static (a relationship or system, for example) or whether you want it to show something dynamic (for example, a process), and plan accordingly. Choose whether you will bring in a visual aid that is already made, or whether you will create the aid in front of the audience (on a flip chart or transparency, for example, or perhaps in response to audience input). Always practice your speech out loud, using (or making) the aid so that you are comfortable handling it.

BRAIN TICKLERS
Set # 33

Think of a visual aid that will enhance your speech. Find it, create it, or plan it, depending on its nature.

(Answers are on page 203.)

How do you know when you're done? (finalization)

As you work through the composing process, as well as preparation and delivery, keep asking yourself if your choices are working toward achieving an utterance. Do you think that when you deliver this speech, you will have said all you wanted to say to this audience at this time, in this context, and that they will be able to respond to you?

BRAIN TICKLERS—THE ANSWERS

Set # 22 through Set # 30

Answers will vary.

Set # 31, page 198

Answers will vary. **Possible response:** I was stirred deeply by the quotation President Reagan used to end his speech.

Set # 32 and Set # 33

Answers will vary.

CHAPTER FIVE

Practicing and Performing "Think All You Speak"

"Think all you speak, but speak not all you think. Your thoughts are your own; your words are so no more."

—Dean Patrick Delany

Irish Clergyman (1685?–1768), Dean of Down

This chapter provides both general, all-purpose advice about speaking and speaking preparation, as well as detailed and specific hints for specialized speaking situations, including reading aloud in the classroom, job interviews, and auditions. It concludes with some suggestions for evaluation that will help you to use each speaking occasion to improve your abilities.

PRACTICING PREPARED MATERIAL

Unrehearsed speaking to others, such as conversation, is a natural part of life. But performance is natural too—look at young children and how they carry on when company comes to visit. Understanding and learning techniques that enhance communication in presentation situations does not make our communication artificial, any more than taking tennis lessons makes our natural athletic abilities phony. Learning to use our body and voice for communication allows us to communicate more deliberately, and thus to have more control over our utterances.

To be effective, rehearsals should be as authentic as possible, so for the most part, practice for performance should be done out loud. Research has shown the value of silently visualizing your performance prior to the event; nevertheless, oral performance requires oral practice.

Stance

Our voices depend on air, and our posture determines how effectively air can move through our bodies. It is best to practice in whatever position you will take when you perform, usually standing or sitting. Since most public speaking is done standing, here is a description of a starting posture, given with the understanding that you will change or adapt to suit your needs.

Stand with your feet under your hips and your weight balanced on both feet. If you wish, you may place one foot slightly in front of the other and put slightly more weight on the forward foot. You don't need to stand stiffly, but you should hold yourself at your full height. Your hands may hang loosely at your sides or you can hold your notes in one hand.

When you need to see your notes, lift them into your line of sight so that you do not have to bend your head. If possible (and if you're comfortable holding your notes), avoid using a podium or stand because it puts a large obstacle between you and your audience. If you must speak from behind a stand, position your notes where you can see them easily and make sure they're in good light.

Breathing

In order for you to speak, you need air. Try this: Inhale and speak at the same time. You can't make very much sound, can you? That's because you need air to be moving outward and vibrating the vocal cords to make speech sounds (see page 9). Now, exhale as much as you can, out of both your nose and your mouth, and then try to speak. You probably can't produce a sound with much quality because you don't have much air left. You not only need air, but you need it in quantity to make quality sound, so take good full breaths.

For your breath to work for you, it has to come from deep inside you. Some people make the mistake of breathing from the throat instead of the diaphragm. Try this exercise in breathing deeply.

Place your notes on the seat of a chair that is moderately heavy. Lift the chair, hold it at arm's length, breathe, and begin your speech. Pay attention to what your breathing feels like. Put down the chair and try to breathe in the same way as you continue speaking.

Also try to make your breathing as inaudible as possible. Especially if you're going to be using a microphone, you don't want people focusing on your breathing noises. Hisses and squeaks can be caused by breathing in through both the nose and mouth and by the position of the mouth when breathing. If you shape your mouth as if you were going to say *eat* and breathe in, you'll probably hear some noise. Try it. Now, shape your mouth to say *oh* and try breathing in again. What do you hear? You should hear less noise, maybe silence.

If you are reading aloud, you may find it helpful to read ahead a few words. This and practicing will help you plan places to breathe that fit naturally with the text—natural pauses for meaning, often those marked by punctuation marks are best.

If you need to, review the section on punctuation in Chapter Three (pages 111–114 and 130–131). You may find it helpful to mark breathing spots.

BRAIN TICKLERS
Set # 34

Try out the breathing exercises. Can you breathe silently?

(Answers are on page 236.)

General speaking drills

If our utterances are to have any effect, our individual words must be understood. Good **enunciation**, or **articulation**, shapes our words with care so that others can interpret our speech easily. Here are some speech drills to help you develop clear and accurate enunciation. For the best results, do the starred exercises with someone who doesn't know what you're reading and see if s/he can understand you.

HARD TO READ
Slowly read a piece of writing, hitting the hard consonant sounds (*b*, *ch*, *d*, *g*, *k*, *p*, and *t*) and overenunciating each syllable. Start slowly, and build up speed. You can try these two nursery rhymes:

Hickety, pickety, my black hen,
She lays eggs for gentlemen.
Gentlemen come every day
To see what my black hen doth lay,
Sometimes nine and sometimes ten.
Hickety, pickety, my black hen.

Hickory, dickory, dock.
A mouse ran up the clock.
The clock struck one,
The mouse ran down.
Hickory, dickory, dock.

PENCIL DRILL*
Read a piece of writing with a pencil
placed horizontally between your teeth.

BUBBLE GUM FUN*
Chew about five sticks of chewing
gum at once and try to read aloud at
the same time. You'll discover just
how clearly you can speak. No fair
sticking the gum in your cheek!

SDRAWKCAB LLIRD
Try reading backward, word by word.
Then read the same material forward.

READING A IS A FUN A
Say the word *a* /uh/ after each word to help prevent slurring.

TONGUE TWISTERS
Here's a fun way to increase your verbal agility. The one-liners
come first, followed by tongue-twisting poems.

> Black background, brown background
> Eddie edited it.
> Flash message!
> Green glass globes glow greenly.
> Lovely lemon liniment.
> Roberta ran rings around the Roman ruins.
> Rubber baby buggy bumpers.
> Six sleek swans swam swiftly southwards.
> Stupid superstition!
> The great Greek grape growers grow great Greek grapes.
> The sixth sick sheik's sixth sheep's sick.
> Three short sword sheaths.
> Toy boat. Toy boat. Toy boat.
> Two toads, totally tired, tried to trot to Tetsbury.
> World Wide Web.

Betty Botter

Betty Botter had some butter
"But," she said, "this butter's bitter
If I bake this bitter butter
it would make my batter bitter.
But a bit of better butter—
that would make my batter better."

So she bought a bit of butter
better than her bitter butter,
and she baked it in her batter,
and the batter was not bitter.
So 'twas better Betty Botter
bought a bit of better butter.

The Night-Light

You've no need to light a night-light
On a light night like tonight.
For a night-light's light's a slight light,
And tonight's a night that's light.
When a night's light, like tonight's light
It is really not quite right
To light night-lights with their slight lights
On a light night like tonight.

The Thistle-Sifter

Theophiles Thistle, the successful thistle-sifter,
in sifting a sieve full of un-sifted thistles,
thrust three thousand thistles through the thick of his thumb.

Now . . . if Theophiles Thistle, the successful thistle-sifter,
in sifting a sieve full of un-sifted thistles,
thrust three thousand thistles through the thick of his thumb,
see that thou, in sifting a sieve full of un-sifted thistles,
thrust not three thousand thistles through the thick of thy thumb.
Success to the successful thistle-sifter!

The Toads

A tree toad loved a she-toad
Who lived up in a tree.
He was a two-toed tree toad
But a three-toed toad was she.
The two-toed tree toad tried to win
The three-toed she-toad's heart,
For the two-toed tree toad loved the ground
That the three-toed tree toad trod.
But the two-toed tree toad tried in vain.
He couldn't please her whim.
From her tree toad bower
With her three-toed power
The she-toad vetoed him.

BRAIN TICKLERS
Set # 35

Try out the enunciation exercises. Which work best for you?

(Answers are on page 236.)

Mirror or recording

Speech experts often advise people to practice speaking while looking in the mirror. This practice may or may not work for you. It's good for focusing your attention on habitual postures, gestures, and other body language that may distract your audience or that you just might not like. After all, you want your audience's attention focused on what you say to them, not drawn to your tapping foot. But looking into one's own eyes can be disconcerting, and it really isn't much like interacting with an audience. With this in mind, you may want to put on the outfit you intend to wear and practice in the mirror once or twice to gain awareness of any unconscious habits and have a look at yourself as your audience will see you. After that, try practicing to some sort of an audience, even if it's your goldfish.

If you have the opportunity to be videotaped, by all means take advantage of it. This is easier today than even five or ten years ago because of the video-recording function in many of today's cell phones as well as cameras. You will obtain a much better indication of your performance behavior on video than you will meeting your own gaze in the mirror. You can even do this yourself with a webcam.

Practicing with an audience

If what you're trying to do is communicate with other people, why practice talking to yourself? When you stop and think about it, it really doesn't make much sense. How can you make judgments about the quality of your communication unless and until you try it out on an audience? Even though it won't be the same audience under the same circumstances, it will still begin to let you know if you've achieved an utterance. If the folks listening to you practice can respond to you as you wish, you need to know that. If they can't, well, you need to know that, too! Also, if you have the opportunity, practice at least once in the performance space. This will allow you to become familiar with the "feel" of the space and also the particular sound. If the space was created for performance, your voice may sound very different than it does in a room in a house or in a classroom. Spaces also have different sounds when they are empty and when they are filled with people. Make your practices as similar to the real event as possible.

Transitions

One of the important things to practice with an audience is your transitions. Whether you are reading a story or delivering a speech, you need to keep your audience aware of where in the structure they are. In a well-written story that follows standard form, the audience will have a fairly easy time determining beginning, middle, or end. In a speech, you need to be careful to bring your audience through your structure with you.

- Remember to stress the transition words you built into your notes. These words will help your audience recognize portions of your speech in which you tackle particular tasks.
- A visual aid can summarize or forecast, if appropriate.
- A pause and a breath can help make a transition between major points, as can a change of position in the speaking area or a direct question to the audience.

Eye contact

"One of the most wonderful things in nature is a glance of the eye; it transcends speech; it is the bodily symbol of identity," said Ralph Waldo Emerson. No matter how many words and how thoughtfully you deliver them, your audience wants to meet your eyes. It is not sufficient to look up from your notes occassionally or scan the back of the room. You must meet the gaze of individuals—they must feel your presence and your being and your energy. This is one of the reasons why practicing with an audience is crucial. You can't learn this skill in the mirror.

Response

Before you present your performance to your audience in practice, tell them what you hope to achieve (what we call an utterance): to say everything you wish to say to this audience in this context on this subject at this time to evoke a particular response. When you have finished, ask them to talk about their response(s). True, this is not the audience and context for which you prepared, but you will have some idea of whether or not your utterance is finalized. If they are puzzled, unconvinced, hostile to your ideas, or unmoved by your rhetoric, you may want to rethink, while you have the time.

Timing

Until you've mastered all the points up to here—adjusted your stance and breathing; improved your enunciation; practiced transitions, eye contact, and response with an audience— you're not prepared to make final timing adjustments. When you're pretty sure that you've got it nailed, then you can do your final fine-tuning. And remember, there are not a lot of situations in which running over or under by a couple of minutes is of great consequence. If you are on a strict time limit, use a timer each and every time you practice and get your speech down to the second. If you fear running over, make sure your crucial material is not at the end of your speech where it might get cut out, or make a plan to keep an eye on the time and leave out a specific section in order to jump to the end if time grows short.

BRAIN TICKLERS
Set # 36

Practice your speech with an audience to refine your use of transitions, eye contact, and timing, and to see if you can elicit the response you desire. Write some notes about how practice changes your performance.

(Answers are on page 236.)

Reading

Reading performance may have some striking differences from what we've talked about so far, especially if you are reading a story. You may be seated, rather than standing, with one or two children on your lap, or you may be reading upside down as you hold a picture book on your lap so young children can see it while you're reading. Now that presents some challenges to the average reader! But in these situations, as elsewhere, practice helps, and many picture books are written with embedded rhythm and rhyme that will help make it easy for you to remember large portions of the text, if not the whole thing.

In addition, the voice you use may *not* be your own—because a lot of the time when you read, it may be a better choice to be in character. Developing characters with the voice can be fun, but it is also challenging. The best model is storytellers or readers who convey a whole story themselves (no cast). Jim Dale is particularly adept at creating and keeping separate a wide variety of voices while narrating a story. Listening to his recordings, you can immediately tell which character is speaking. This is another area in which working with an audience in practice can be extremely helpful in knowing how you're doing.

Gesticulation

Gesturing when reading aloud partly depends on what you are reading and partly on whether or not your hands are full of book. If they're not, your hands can help with characterization: you can keep one hand palm down on the book with your forefinger marking your place while you use the other hand, for example, to point, wave, offer, refuse, pat, slap, hit, signal okay, signal "thumbs up," or thumb your nose—whatever gesture would express the character's inner being at that moment.

Action

If you are reading an essay or other expository work, you may well deliver it standing in place. If, however, you are reading a story, and if your lap is not piled with children, you may use your freedom to change positions—you may go from sitting to standing; you may walk, stop, pause, and continue your stroll—whatever motion seems in keeping with the text and adds to your presentation. You can even move among the audience.

Audience interaction

For many people, the first experience of being read to is couched within a conversation with an older person: the book has a place within a broader stream of communication. This creates the sense that being read to is an intimate activity—one in which the interaction is not formal and confined to the task at hand (one reads; the other listens) but is informal and can move from reading into discussion or commentary or questions or joint wondering about the book or about life. For other people, the experience of the story (see Poe's comments on page 136)—the suspension of disbelief and the sense of being in another place, another time, another world—is such an incredible gift that they do not want anything to break into or mar their experience. So you can have, in the same audience, the curious questioners and the eager shushers. For each performance, given the audience and the context, you must weigh the choices and decide if you want to offer the audience continuous interaction, or if you want questions saved for the end. Before you begin, you must make the parameters of the performance clear to the audience. If you are on a proscenium stage, you will have less of a problem encouraging your audience to hold their questions than if you are sitting cross-legged on the floor with them.

BRAIN TICKLERS
Set # 37

Practice reading with an audience to work on gesticulation, action, and audience interaction, as appropriate to your piece. Write some notes about how practice affected your performance decisions.

(Answers are on page 236.)

Speaking

If your speech focuses on a personal experience of high adventure, some of the advice for readers may well fit the bill for you. You may use vocal characterization and gesticulation to bring your story to life for your audience. If you are delivering a more formal speech genre, you are likely to adopt a less mobile voice and stance.

One occasion for a change of voice that you are likely to come across in a formal speech is a quotation. Sometimes a quotation is slipped seamlessly into place without any differentiation. But often it is introduced by a pause and a change of inflection to signal—without saying "and I quote" or "as —— once said" or something similar—that the material that is being said is from a source other than the speaker.

Preparing for audience response

Preparing for audience interaction should be a priority for a speaker. If the point of an utterance is to gain a response, then anticipating audience response is a key element of your preparation. Especially if you are trying to affect people's actions or values, if you can have the opportunity to find out how you did, why not take it?

As a speaker, you can take several different approaches to audience interaction. You can choose to interact directly with the audience from the moment you arrive. If you're speaking to your own class, this will naturally be the case, but if you're speaking to a group of people you don't know, you have a choice of making your speech more or less like a conversation. To foster interaction, you can

- ask the audience direct questions in the course of your speech,
- create opportunities for audience comments (invite them to raise a hand to indicate they have something to say),
- have the audience participate in demonstrations, quizzes, surveys, and the like (how many of you have ever . . . ?),
- allow time for questions and answers after your presentation is complete.

If you are going to allow questions, then prepare yourself for the most difficult questions you can imagine. Is there anything you left out of your speech? Be prepared to answer questions about it. Did you find any evidence that contradicted your thesis? Be ready to explain why you stuck to your ideas in the face of those facts. Other questions you should be ready to answer include:

- Who's your authority?
- Where did you read that?
- What do you mean?
- What's your evidence for that claim?

If you anticipate that you are likely to receive such questions, come to your speech prepared with the answers.

Any time you allow audience participation, you may receive questions that are irrelevant, inappropriate, or beyond the bounds of your subject or knowledge. Such questions should be dealt with calmly and evenly. You need to distinguish carefully between questions that are legitimate, though difficult or put to you by a person who is hostile to your point of view from questions that are out of bounds, even if put by a well-meaning or friendly audience member.

BRAIN TICKLERS
Set # 38

Prepare for audience interaction during and/or after your speech, as appropriate for your situation. What questions do you anticipate? How will you answer them?

(Answers are on page 236.)

How much should I practice?

Whether you are reading aloud or speaking, professionals estimate that you will need four to six run-throughs. Remember that this is only an estimate. Length, complexity of material, or other factors may make you feel that you need even more practice. The best rule is to practice until you feel as comfortable as you can feel in the situation (given time and other constraints). You should know your main points and ideas and feel comfortable expressing them. You'll probably have some phrases that you use every single time, and some that vary. Especially for your first experience, you want to feel that you've made the maximum effort beforehand to ensure success.

DELIVERING PREPARED MATERIAL

What's the difference between a dress rehearsal and the performance? Several things distinguish the two. Do you remember the discussion of performative language on pages 96–97? We treat language in rehearsal as ordinary and language in performance as performative. What we say in performance acquires a power and a meaning and an energy *simply because of the fact that it's in performance.* No matter how smoothly everything goes in rehearsal, it's not the same. Is it partly the anticipation? Or is it the sense of finality—that this is it? Or is it the coming together of all the elements—you, your audience, the occasion? Maybe it's all three.

Speech anxiety or stage fright

That sense of having only one chance can be glorious . . . or terrifying. Some people feel a bit (or very) overwhelmed by public speaking. Just being aware that you may become somewhat unsettled can help you maintain your poise. You should know that the energy that manifests itself in nervousness can be converted into positive vitality and enthusiasm that can energize your performance.

Identifying your concerns can help you address them in a positive way. If you are wary of speaking to strangers, you can do what many speakers do and take the time to greet and get to know a few members of your audience before your presentation begins. When you get up to begin, locate those people, and make a point of making eye contact with them. If you take these steps, you'll have familiar faces to focus on as you talk.

If time constraints concern you, make sure that you arrive early. If you are sensitive to temperature, dress in layers and come early to assess the comfort of the room (keep in mind that rooms warm up as they fill with people). If you are concerned about your throat getting dry, bring a water bottle from which you can discreetly sip before you begin and after you finish. If you are speaking at a public function, you will usually find water provided on the speaker's platform. If not, you may want to ask for it.

Another thing you can do is decide beforehand whether or not you're the type of person who should do a last minute rehearsal or whether you should finish practicing the day before and give yourself a break. Based on your personality, make a decision about the kind of schedule that will help you have the most relaxed approach to your performance.

If you do feel nervous, here are some things that may happen and some actions you can take to help you cope.

COPING WITH SPEECH ANXIETY OR STAGE FRIGHT	
Sign of Nervousness	**What You Can Do**
choppy speech or too quick speech	Tap the toes of one foot inside your shoe in a moderate rhythm and read to the rhythm.
fidgeting hand motions	Depending on your situation: • Lightly rest your hands on the podium; • Hold your hands flat against your sides; • Put one palm down on your notes with your forefinger as an indicator to follow and the other on the edge of the stand.
giggling	Take several deep breaths and avoid making eye contact with a friend who might make you laugh harder.

What to do on the day of your speech

Whether you are reading or doing oral interp or giving a prepared speech, here are some guidelines for the day of your presentation.

Final copy of your notes

The final copy of your notes should be word processed or printed as large as reasonable to make them easy to read while minimizing page turns. If you are placing them on a stand, you can probably count on two sheets resting side by side. Make sure you practice with your final copy at least once so that you know where on the page(s) things are.

What (NOT) to eat

Speech coaches advise that you avoid milk and dairy products prior to public speaking. Cabbage, carbonated beverages, and other foods that can cause burping, as well as very spicy foods, are better avoided. It is also wise to avoid eating immediately before your performance. Plenty of water is recommended, and melon (like cantaloupe) and tart apples are recommended.

What to wear

If you are appearing in character or doing a demonstration, your outfit should reflect those requirements. Otherwise, your attire should reflect the formality of the occasion and your relationship with the audience. In any case, you should choose your clothes well in advance and wear them during practice to make sure that they work with any movements you have incorporated.

Where to stand or sit

The exact place to stand or sit may be predetermined and obvious when you reach the performance space. If you have a choice, you should judge by both sound and sight. Test the sound in the performance space, if you haven't had a chance to practice there. Begin saying your piece. You want to have the best sound and still be in everyone's line of sight. Consider the type of visual aid(s) you are using. Do you need to be near a projector control? Do you need a place against which to lean your visual aid? Do you want to have an array of items in front of you that you can point to? Make your choices based on your particular presentation.

Timing

If you need to keep to a strict time, and you are unsure of the length of your presentation, ask a friend to sit in a visible spot in the audience and act as a timekeeper for you. At a preset warn-ing time, your friend should discreetly raise his or her hand to signal you and then signal you again when your maximum time limit is reached. This will make it possible for you to focus on your speech and not on a stopwatch.

Watch your audience

Whether or not you have decided to allow your audience to speak during your presentation, you can allow them to give you feedback by watching their faces and body language. Are they smiling, thoughtful, perplexed, curious, engaged? Do you feel that they are "with you"? If you discover that your audience is different than you expected (in a really good mood, more sophisticated or thoughtful than you'd anticipated, or already attuned to the issue about which you're speaking), you may want to change some of your remarks or to address the matter directly. For example, "I see by your reactions that many of you have more than a passing familiarity with the development of children's theatre in America, so I'm going to move on to some recent innovations in the use of multimedia in children's theatre."

Stand and deliver

There are two basic and very different ideas about public speaking. One is that the goal of public speaking is to say something original—that you may take the same old subject but use your creativity to put a new twist on the way it's perceived. The second idea is that everything's already been said but not by you. It's not what you say that matters anyway; it's how you say it, and because you are unique, you will say things in a unique manner.

I actually think both can be true. I would argue that even "I love you"—probably the most repeated phrase in human existence (if you count it in all languages)—is absolutely unique in every occurrence because the *I* and the *you* that exist in this moment have never existed before (and will never exist again), so the thought and the utterance are unrepeatable. I and you will both be changed by that utterance and be different from then on.

John Campbell wrote in *Speech Preparation* (1981, p. 41): "A speech is an incarnation, an idea in flesh—personality and personal contact are its very lifeblood." You used your mind when you thought about the ideas for your speech. Now you are going to use your body to convey those ideas to an audience. Whatever has happened in practice is one thing. Now is the utterance.

BRAIN TICKLERS
Set # 39

Are your final preparations complete for your performance? Create a checklist for yourself to help you next time you present. What do you need to do (and when) in order to make your preparation smooth and comfortable?

(Answers are on page 236.)

WINGING IT

If you have ever prepared for a reading or a speech, all that preparation wasn't just for that one event. No, all that work carries over, not only into the next reading or speech but also into all the unrehearsed reading and speaking you do.

Reading on the spot

Whether you're reading a story to a child you are baby-sitting, reading aloud a newspaper account of your brother's latest sports triumph to amuse your friends, or auditioning for a play, there you are with little or no time to prepare, trying not only to make sense of somebody else's words and guess where they're going but also maybe to create a character at the same time. That takes skill—and quick thinking! It can be especially challenging if you're reading with others (see page 149) who aren't keeping up their end of things. If you're feeling frustrated, keep in mind that reading out loud is not a skill that has been widely taught. If your fellow readers are having difficulties, your best strategy may be to imagine that they are doing the best they can.

Auditions

Acting is a process of creating a character, often one based on a script. When you act, the idea is to give the illusion that what you are doing is happening for the first time every time you perform it.

At an audition, you (and perhaps some other actors) are usually in street clothes and may read prepared lines or lines you have never seen before. This is called a *cold reading,* or—if you are given no preparation time whatsoever—an *ice cold reading.* The array of talent at an audition is just that—an array. You could be reading with someone who has loads of talent or not— you never know. So while an audition may be the checkpoint you have to pass in many cases in order to act, what you have to be able to do in an audition requires some different skills than what you need to do as an actor.

Simply put, in a nonprofessional audition, these are the most important things in order:

1. How you enter the audition space (3 seconds);
2. How you walk to your spot where you will perform (10 seconds);
3. How you say your name (3 seconds);
4. If you *look* the part;
5. The material you perform (2 minutes most likely);
6. Your craft as an actor (plus any innate talent).

There are techniques for all of this, but the first 20 seconds are the most important, believe it or not.

If you are doing a prepared reading, it is generally a monologue—a speech for one character from some play, chosen to show the best you can do. The hints for reading aloud in Chapter 3, and for preparing in this chapter, as well as any acting instruction and coaching you have had will help you with your monologue.

But, you may have to do a cold reading, a monologue or scene that you have never read before, in which case you will only have a few minutes to look at the scene. Here are some hints:

- Read through the whole scene. Think about your charac- ter. Ask yourself briefly about the Five W's surrounding your character's situation—Who, What, When, Where, and Why? Answer these questions (as far as you can): What are my character's age, ethnic background, profession, beliefs, interests, economic status? What is his or her life situa- tion? Who are the significant people in his or her life?

- Read through once more. Think about the scene in terms of beginning, middle, and end. Answer these questions: What is the focus of the scene? What is my character's goal for this scene? What obstacles stand in the way? What is the central conflict? What happened just before this scene that precipitated this scene's action?
- Look for the key words. In each line, mark the word that should have the most stress. Mark pauses.

- Learn to "grab a line" and look up from the script to deliver it directly to your scene partner.
- When you do the reading, hold the book or papers in one hand. Follow the lines with the forefinger of your dominant hand.
- When your audition is complete, thank the director.

Reading texts in the classroom

Teachers sometimes cover material in class by having students read it aloud. This can give teachers the assurance that the text has been covered, lessen homework time for students, and—for certain types of literature (e.g., scripts)—allow students to experience works in a manner that is closer to their originally intended purpose than they would if they each read the work silently. It does, however, mean that students do some ice cold readings. Here are some hints on how to get the most out of this kind of experience.

- If you know you aren't good at ice cold readings and you're going to have to do them, practice. It doesn't have to be extremely painful. You can use your favorite magazine, and for one article, instead of reading silently, read it out loud. For practice in doing characters, read comic strips. Preface each character's lines by saying, "Then <name> said."
- Think about your own learning. Reading aloud is primarily an aural experience. Are you an aural learner? If so, you're likely to benefit a lot from listening to your classmates. If not, here's a chance to strengthen a weaker area in your repertoire.
- If you're reading in a subject area, note the topic carefully. Look for key words (often boldfaced or printed in color) and stress them. Read at a moderate pace with distinct enunciation.
- If you're reading a script or a work of fiction, you can try to do some vocal characterization to make your part more meaningful. Remember that you can use all the flexibility and variation in the voice (pitch, volume, tempo, tone, stress, and pauses/silence) to create character. If you're reading a script, look ahead for your character's next line and note the **cue** (the line before yours). If you're reading fiction, look carefully to see who's speaking before you begin to characterize the dialogue.
- If you're reading a poem, quickly identify the use of sound (like rhymes) and meter. See if you can identify the speaker. Use punctuation, not the end of lines, to judge where pauses should be.

Unrehearsed speaking

Unrehearsed speaking is closely related to prepared speech. You follow some of the same preparation steps, only more quickly, and you limit your subjects to those about which you can speak from your existing knowledge with little or no time for research and no rehearsal. Several different formats are followed. In one, you choose your own topic. In another, the audience proposes several topics, from which you may select one. The characteristic features are the sudden proposal to speak and the minimal preparation time. In any case, you can follow these steps:

1. Quickly assess the audience (page 165) and consider your favorite speech genres (page 170). Using those choices as guides, choose a subject (pages 171–172) and purpose for your utterance.
2. Create a thesis statement (pages 182–183). Write it down.
3. Organize your talk by identifying tasks and major supporting points (page 186). Note them in outline form, leaving room above and below for your introduction and conclusion.
4. Brainstorm an introduction and conclusion. Note them briefly in your outline (see pages 196 and 197).
5. Choose a title (page 198). Write it at the top of your outline.
6. Stand up, gather your audience's attention, and deliver your speech. Robert F. Kennedy's speech (page 256) is an unrehearsed speech.

Answering questions in class

You may have a whole new perspective on answering questions in class if you think of the questions (when appropriate) as mini-tasks using the task analysis on page 179 and compose your answers accordingly. If you are a visual learner, you may even picture one of the graphic organizers in your mind's eye and run through it as you speak.

Oral examinations

Many people have never experienced an oral examination. For those who feel challenged taking written examinations and are more comfortable speaking, oral examinations can be a welcome change. You just demonstrate your knowledge in a different mode.

Here are some hints for doing well in an oral examination:

- Write out a list of questions that you think you may be asked and practice with a friend. For each question, identify the answer with a task type/relationship/graphic organizer (see page 179), and use that structure to organize your answer. Think about creating a finalized utterance for each answer.

At the exam:

- If you don't receive questions in advance, listen carefully to each question and focus only on it. You may repeat it, if that helps you to be sure that you have understood. If you are unclear about what is required of you, ask for clarification before you begin your answer.
- Unlike a written examination, where you are graded only on what is on your paper, in an oral examination, your attitude, posture, attire, level of formality, eye contact, and poise all contribute to the impression you create because they are part of your communication.
- If you do not know an answer, say so plainly. If you have something pertinent to add, such as how you would find it out (I know that to solve this problem I need to apply the formula for projectile motion, but I have forgotten it), do so briefly.
- Unlike a written examination, in which the questions are set before you arrive, the questions in an oral examination are often formulated based on your performance. The examiner will question you to test the limits of your knowledge. Therefore, unlike a written examination, on which you may achieve a perfect score, you are likely to receive questions that you are unable to answer in an oral examination. If you have mastered the material you were supposed to cover, don't think of not knowing something outside your preparation area as failure; it is not like leaving a blank on a written exam, and it does not mean that you will not do well.

Improvisation

Improvisation is unscripted theatre that usually springs from a set of *given circumstances*, a term that comes from Stanislavski and refers to the starting situation, characters, and action that are defined for an improv. Although actors create dialogue and actions spontaneously as they improvise—with the result that the world created by the actors tends to transform quickly sometimes—changes need to make sense within the imaginary world they're creating. Improvisation requires shared assumptions. The actors and the audience all agree to accept each actor's contributions as real for the sake of the fun to be had by all.

Improv is a valued learning tool, used for many years by teachers in the classroom and by directors in rehearsal. **Spot improv**, a more recent development, uses suggestions from an audience to prompt the creation of short, entertaining scenes. There are many, well-tested improv systems and improv-based theatre games available in books and on the Internet. Check the *Painless Speaking* website for links to improv games.

Meetings

Meetings often combine prepared presentations with impromptu question-and-answer sessions. You can treat this type of meeting much like an oral examination, and remember that a speech is a speech is a speech—you can prepare using the same guidelines for a meeting as for other speaking opportunities.

Job interviews

Job interviews are also like oral examinations, but they are nearly always formal and are usually characterized by a highly predictable set of questions for which you can prepare yourself. Here are some of the standard questions that you may expect to be asked, depending on your age and experience. To get more comfortable with them, have a friend ask you the questions, and answer them as carefully as you can. Ask for feedback, and revise your answers. As in oral examinations, treat each question as a minitask. Frame it for yourself in a structure, and make sure that your utterance is finalized.

- Tell me about yourself. (Best answer: What would you like to know?)
- What type of position are you interested in? or What is your ideal job?
- What led you to decide to seek a position with this company?
- What salary do you want to make in this job?
- Where do you see yourself five years from now?
- If you are hired, how long do you plan to stay with this company?
- How do you explain gaps in your work history? low grades? terminations? a lay-off?
- What is your greatest weakness?
- What is your greatest asset or strength?
- What do you bring to this company that we will not find in any other candidate?
- In what context have you given your best? How could we help you give your best if you worked for this company?
- How do you handle stress?
- How do you deal with difficult people?
- Tell me about a time when you received criticism for your work or an idea.
- What have you done that shows initiative?
- How do you approach working in groups? Do you tend to play a particular role?
- Describe the positive and the negative aspects of your previous job.
- Why do you think you would enjoy this kind of work?
- What do I not know about you that would help me make my decision?
- Do you have any questions?

Always thank the interviewer before you leave. You should have an expectation of when you might hear back from the company about whether you have gotten the job or the next round of interviews.

EVALUATING SPEECH

It is likely that many of your presentations will receive informal or formal evaluation—anything from the audience's applause to a letter grade from a teacher or professor. But it's a good idea for you to evaluate your own performance, regardless of how others perceive it. You can use any rating system that suits you such as 1–5 stars, letter grades, or + or −.

EVALUATION FORM FOR PERFORMANCE		
Criteria	**Rating**	**Notes For Next Time**
End Result		
Achieved finalized utterance • communication said all you wanted to say in the place and time on the given subject and was appropriate to context and audience and was answerable		
Audience responded as desired • act • feel • think • commit to, value		
Composition		
Introduction caught attention		
Body supported thesis • accurate • complete • specific • authoritative • relevant • logical		

EVALUATION FORM FOR PERFORMANCE, cont.		
Criteria	**Rating**	**Notes For Next Time**
Body organization served well • good transitions • identifiable tasks		
Conclusion ended effectively		
Language use		
Appropriate speech genre • unified presentation		
Delivery		
Vocal expression • enunciation • rate • flow • stress • pauses • characterization		
Bodily action		
Gesticulation		
Eye contact		
Paralanguage (facial expression, etc.)		
Appropriate use of visual aid(s) and equipment		
Poise		
Audience interaction handled gracefully		

© Copyright 2003 by Mary Elizabeth.

You can find a file of this chart on the *Painless Speaking* website at http://www.edreinvented.com/products/painless-speaking

There is a proverb that says, "Words are the only things that last forever." If they're going to last so long, we may as well send them out into the air bearing valuable, true, funny, vibrant, vital thoughts. What do you say?

BRAIN TICKLERS—THE ANSWERS

Set # 34, page 209

Answers will vary. **Possible response:** Yes.

Set # 35, page 212

Answers will vary. **Possible response:** Because I tend to slur my words, putting *a* between each word helped my speaking.

Set # 36 through Set # 39

Answers will vary.

Appendices

APPENDIX A—GRAPHIC ORGANIZERS

Introduction to graphic organizers

The following collection of graphic organizers is labeled and organized to match the chart on page 179. This is to help you choose appropriate graphic organizers as you are brainstorming and creating a speech.

However, each graphic organizer is also labeled with the task type that it is associated with, and this allows you to easily use them to create well-structured answers to questions in an interview or create targeted portions of a piece of writing that is not forming the basis of a speech. Here is a mini Table of Contents to help you find what you need:

Comparative analysis

Use either of these graphic organizers to compare and contrast, or modify them to show only differences or opposition, on the one hand, or only similarities, on the other.

Compare/Contrast Type 1—Venn Diagram

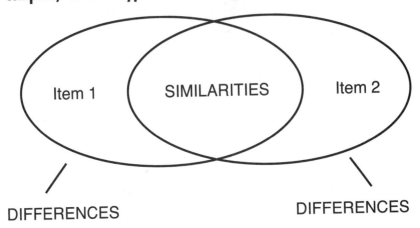

Compare/Contrast Type 2—Attribute Lists

Item 1   Item 2

SIMILARITIES

DIFFERENCES

Operational analysis

Use Define/Describe Type 1 to explain the stages of an operation or process occurring over time. Use Define/Describe Type 2 to show a more complex set of functions, modifying it as necessary.

Define/Describe Type 1—Process

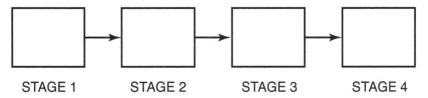

STAGE 1   STAGE 2   STAGE 3   STAGE 4

Define/Describe Type 2—Flow Chart

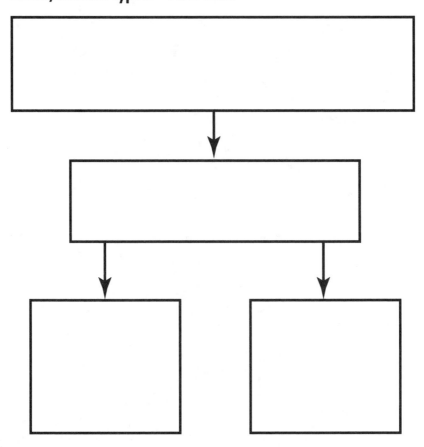

Structural analysis

Use Define/Describe Type 3 to show the structure of something, substituting *parts* for *systems* if it makes sense to do so.

Define/Describe Type 3—Concept

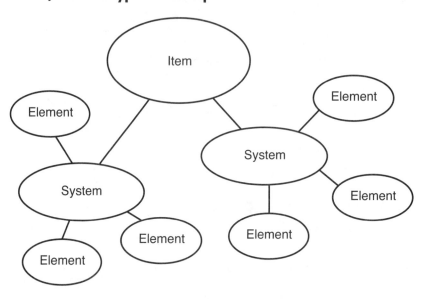

Sensory analysis

Use Define/Describe Type 4—often called a "spider diagram"— to organize a sensory description of something's attributes.

Define/Describe Type 4—Spider Diagram

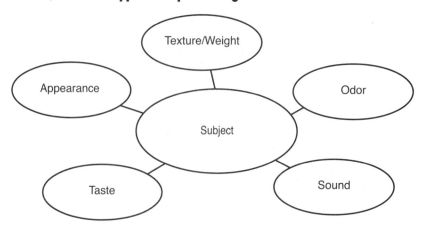

Relational analysis

Use Define/Describe Type 5 to show how your subject interacts with its associates, modifying the diagram to show the number and type of relationships and whether the things it relates to are similar or different.

Define/Describe Type 5—Interaction

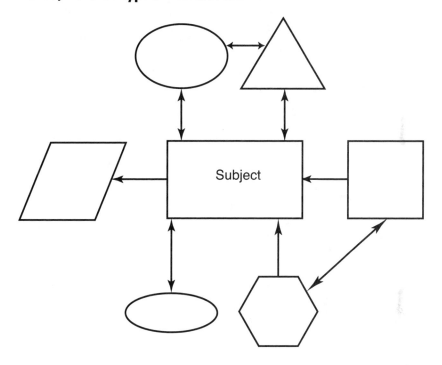

Theoretical, meaning, or thematic analysis

Use Define/Describe Type 6 to show how you came to determine the meaning or theme of something.

Define/Describe Type 6 — Find Meaning/Theme

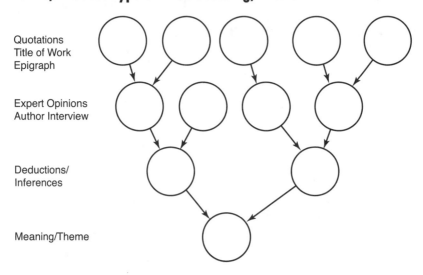

Utilization analysis

Use Define/Describe Type 7 to record the various uses to which something can be put or the purposes for which it was designed.

Define/Describe Type 7 — Uses

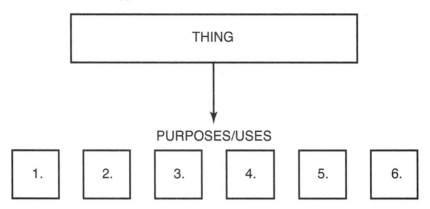

Evaluative analysis

Use Define/Describe Type 8 to record the criteria by which something is customarily or can be evaluated, and then add the scoring or rating that you give it and explain why in your summary.

Define/Describe Type 8—Rubric

CRITERIA	RATING
1.	
2.	
3.	
4.	
SUMMARY	

Situational analysis

Use Define/Describe Type 9 to show an analysis of the impact its environment has on something. To show your subject's impact on its environment, turn the arrows around, or if they interact, use a double-headed arrow.

Define/Describe Type 9—Modified Spider

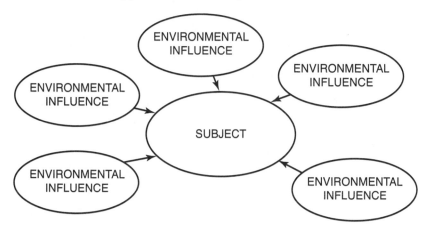

Logical analysis

Use the Argue Type 1 graphic organizer to show a hypothesis and its support. Use Type 2 to show a proposition and its support or a statement and its proof. Use Type 3 for a question and answer.

Argue Type 1—Hypothesis

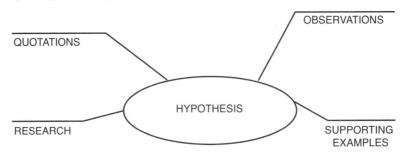

Argue Type 2—Proposition/Support or Statement/Proof

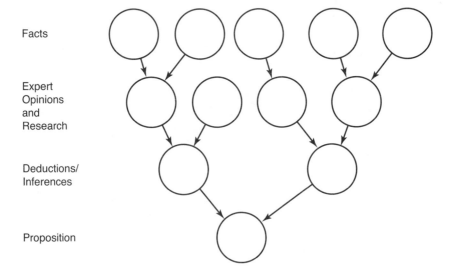

Argue Type 3—Question/Answer

Question: _____
_____

Answer: _____
_____

↑

Supporting Details:

1.

2.

3.

Problem/solution analysis

Use Argue Type 4 to show the complexities of solving a problem.

Argue Type 4 — Problem/Solution

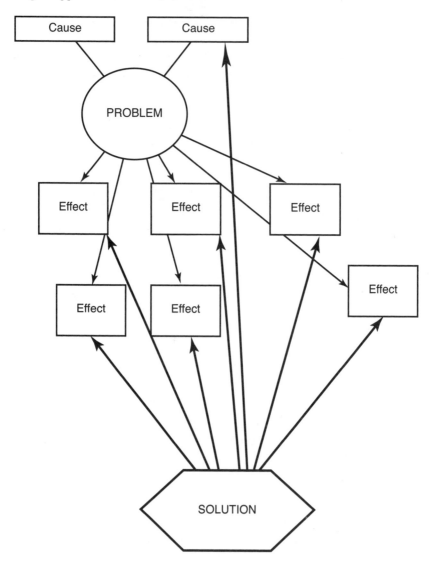

Cause/effect, response, or emotional analysis

Use either Narrate/Sequence Type1 graphic organizer to show what led up to an effect, response, or emotion. The second example allows you to show more complexity.

Narrate/Sequence Type 1 — Fishbone

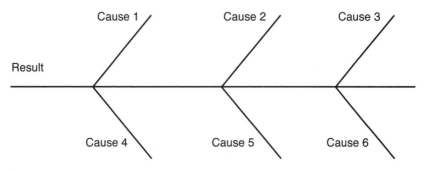

Narrate/Sequence Type 1 — Cause/Effect with Levels

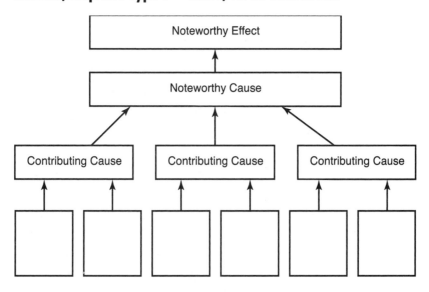

Historical analysis

Use any of the Narrate/Sequence Type 2 graphic organizers to show events over time, either a chain with a single event at a time or a multi-event depiction.

Narrate/Sequence Type 2—Succession of Events

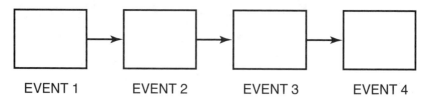

EVENT 1   EVENT 2   EVENT 3   EVENT 4

Narrate/Sequence Type 2—Succession of Events

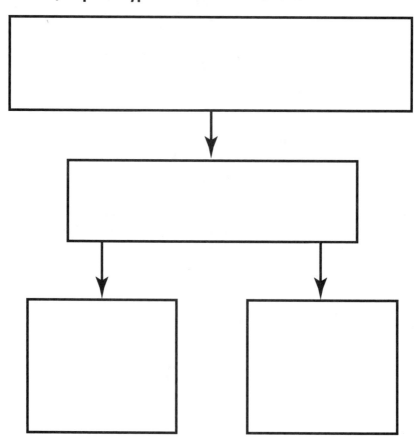

Narrate/Sequence Type 2—Timeline

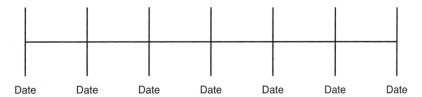

Date   Date   Date   Date   Date   Date   Date

Classification analysis

Use Classify/Categorize Type 1 to show a hierarchy and/or how your subject fits into the larger scheme of things.

Classify/Categorize Type 1—Hierarchy

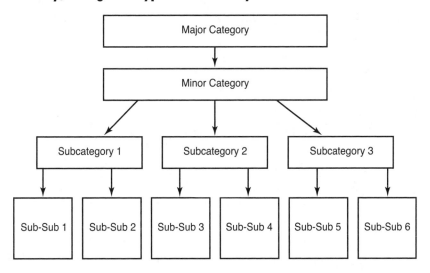

APPENDIX B—SELECTED SPEECHES

Here are some great speeches from American history that you may wish to read and study. Listening to or watching famous speeches after becoming familiar with the text is an especially valuable tool to hone your public speaking skills.

Ain't I a Woman?

Sojourner Truth (1797–1883) delivered this address to the Women's Convention in Akron, Ohio, in 1851.

Well, children, where there is so much racket there must be something out of kilter. I think that 'twixt the negroes of the South and the women at the North, all talking about rights, the white men will be in a fix pretty soon. But what's all this here talking about?

That man over there says that women need to be helped into carriages, and lifted over ditches, and to have the best place everywhere. Nobody ever helps me into carriages, or over mud-puddles, or gives me any best place! And ain't I a woman? Look at me! Look at my arm! I have ploughed and planted, and gathered into barns, and no man could head me! And ain't I a woman? I could work as much and eat as much as a man— when I could get it—and bear the lash as well! And ain't I a woman? I have borne thirteen children, and seen most all sold off to slavery, and when I cried out with my mother's grief, none but Jesus heard me! And ain't I a woman?

Then they talk about this thing in the head; what's this they call it? [Member of audience whispers, "intellect."] That's it, honey. What's that got to do with women's rights or negroes' rights? If my cup won't hold but a pint, and yours holds a quart, wouldn't you be mean not to let me have my little half measure full?

Then that little man in black there, he says women can't have as much rights as men, 'cause Christ wasn't a woman! Where did your Christ come from? Where did your Christ come from? From God and a woman! Man had nothing to do with Him.

If the first woman God ever made was strong enough to turn the world upside down all alone, these women together ought to be able to turn it back, and get it right side up again! And now they is asking to do it, the men better let them.

Obliged to you for hearing me, and now old Sojourner ain't got nothing more to say.

The Gettysburg Address

On November 19, 1863, President Abraham Lincoln dedicated the Union cemetery at Gettysburg with this speech.

Four score and seven years ago our fathers brought forth on this continent a new nation, conceived in liberty and dedicated to the proposition that all men are created equal.

Now we are engaged in a great civil war, testing whether that nation or any nation so conceived and so dedicated can long endure. We are met on a great battlefield of that war. We have come to dedicate a portion of that field as a final resting-place for those who here gave their lives that that nation might live. It is altogether fitting and proper that we should do this.

But in a larger sense, we cannot dedicate, we cannot consecrate, we cannot hallow this ground. The brave men, living and dead, who struggled here have consecrated it far above our poor power to add or detract.

The world will little note nor long remember what we say here, but it can never forget what they did here. It is for us the living rather to be dedicated here to the unfinished work which they who fought here have thus far so nobly advanced. It is rather for us to be here dedicated to the great task remaining before us—that from these honored dead we take increased devotion to that cause for which they gave the last full measure of devotion—that we here highly resolve that these dead shall not have died in vain, that this nation under God shall have a new birth of freedom, and that government of the people, by the people, for the people shall not perish from the earth.

I Will Fight No More Forever

Chief Joseph of the Nez Perce (1840?–1904), known as "Thunder Traveling to the Loftier Mountain Heights," led the resistance against the takeover of Nez Perce lands by white settlers in Oregon. Ordered to move to a reservation in Idaho in 1877, Chief Joseph agreed at first, but after members of his tribe fought several battles with the U.S. Army as they tried to flee to Canada, Chief Joseph surrendered with this speech on October 5, 1877.

Tell General Howard I know his heart. What he told me before, I have it in my heart. I am tired of fighting. Our Chiefs are killed; Looking Glass is dead, Ta Hool Hool Shute is dead. The old men are all dead. It is the young men who say yes or no. He who led on the young men is dead. It is cold, and we have no blankets; the little children are freezing to death. My people, some of them, have run away to the hills, and have no blankets, no food. No one knows where they are—perhaps freezing to death. I want to have time to look for my children, and see how many of them I can find. Maybe I shall find them among the dead. Hear me, my Chiefs! I am tired; my heart is sick and sad. From where the sun now stands I will fight no more forever.

William Faulkner's Nobel Prize Acceptance Speech

Upon accepting the Nobel Prize in literature in Stockholm, Sweden, on December 10, 1950, American Novelist William Faulkner presented this address.

I feel that this award was not made to me as a man, but to my work—a life's work in the agony and sweat of the human spirit, not for glory and least of all for profit, but to create out of the materials of the human spirit something which did not exist before. So this award is only mine in trust. It will not be difficult to find a dedication for the money part of it commensurate with the purpose and significance of its origin. But I would like to do the same with the acclaim too, by using this moment as a pinnacle from which I might be listened to by the young men and women already dedicated to the same anguish and travail, among whom is already that one who will some day stand where I am standing.

Our tragedy today is a general and universal physical fear so long sustained by now that we can even bear it. There are no longer problems of the spirit. There is only one question: When will I be blown up? Because of this, the young man or woman writing today has forgotten the problems of the human heart in conflict with itself which alone can make good writing because only that is worth writing about, worth the agony and the sweat.

He must learn them again. He must teach himself that the basest of all things is to be afraid: and, teaching himself that, forget it forever, leaving no room in his workshop for anything but the old verities and truths of the heart, the universal truths lacking which any story is ephemeral and doomed—love and honor and pity and pride and compassion and sacrifice. Until he does so, he labors under a curse. He writes not of love but of lust, of defeats in which nobody loses anything of value, of victories without hope and, worst of all, without pity or compassion. His griefs grieve on no universal bones, leaving no scars. He writes not of the heart but of the glands.

Until he learns these things, he will write as though he stood among and watched the end of man. I decline to accept the end of man. It is easy enough to say that man is immortal simply because he will endure: that when the last ding-dong of doom has clanged and faded from the last worthless rock hanging tideless in the last red and dying evening, that even then there will still be one more sound: that of his inexhaustible voice, still talking. I refuse to accept this. I believe that man will not merely endure: he will prevail. He is immortal, not because he alone among creatures has an inexhaustible voice, but because he has a soul, a spirit capable of compassion and sacrifice and endurance. The poet's, the writer's, duty is to write about these things. It is his privilege to help man endure by lifting his heart, by reminding him of the courage and honor and hope and pride and compassion and pity and sacrifice which have been the glory of his past. The poet's voice need not merely be the record of man, it can be one of the props, the pillars to help him endure and prevail.

Robert F. Kennedy Eulogizes Dr. Martin Luther King, Jr.

At a political rally supporting his campaign for the Democratic presidential nomination on April 4, 1968, Robert F. Kennedy realized that the crowd was unaware that Dr. Martin Luther King, Jr. had been assassinated and made this impromptu announcement.

Do they know about Martin Luther King? [speaking to a rally organizer]

Man in crowd: No. We've left that up to you.

Kennedy: Could you lower those signs, please? [People lower their "RFK for President" picket-signs.]

I have bad news for you, for all of our fellow citizens, and people who love peace all over the world, and that is that Martin Luther King was shot and killed tonight.

Martin Luther King dedicated his life to love and to justice for his fellow human beings, and he died because of that effort.

In this difficult day, in this difficult time for the United States, it is perhaps well to ask what kind of a nation we are and what direction we want to move in. For those of you who are black— considering the evidence there evidently is, that there were white people who were responsible—you can be filled with bitterness, with hatred, and a desire for revenge. We can move in that direction as a country, in great polarization—black people amongst black, white people amongst white, filled with hatred toward one another.

Or we can make an effort, as Martin Luther King did, to understand and to comprehend, and to replace that violence, that stain of blood shed that has spread across our land, with an effort to understand with compassion and love.

For those of you who are black and are tempted to be filled with hatred and distrust at the injustice of such an act, against all white people, I can only say that I feel in my own heart that same kind of feeling. I had a member of my family killed, but he was killed by a white man. But we have to make an effort in the United States, we have to make an effort to understand, to go beyond these rather difficult times.

My favorite poet was Aeschylus. He wrote: "In our sleep, pain which cannot forget falls drop by drop upon the heart until, in our own despair, against our will, comes wisdom through the awful grace of God."

What we need in the United States is not division; what we need in the United States is not hatred; what we need in the United States is not violence or lawlessness; but love and wisdom, and compassion toward one another, and a feeling of justice toward those who still suffer within our country, whether they be white or they be black.

So I shall ask you tonight to return home, to say a prayer for the family of Martin Luther King, that's true, but more importantly, to say a prayer for our own country, which all of us love—a prayer for understanding and that compassion of which I spoke.

We can do well in this country. We will have difficult times; we've had difficult times in the past; we will have difficult times in the future. It is not the end of violence; it is not the end of lawlessness; it is not the end of disorder.

But the vast majority of white people and the vast majority of black people in this country want to live together, want to improve the quality of our life, and want justice for all human beings who abide in our land.

Let us dedicate ourselves to what the Greeks wrote so many years ago: to tame the savageness of man and make gentle the life of this world.

Let us dedicate ourselves to that, and say a prayer for our country and for our people.

Tribute to the Challenger *Astronauts*

On January 28, 1986, the Space Shuttle Challenger *exploded shortly after takeoff from Cape Kennedy, killing all seven astronauts aboard, including New Hampshire teacher Christa McAuliffe. President Ronald Reagan addressed the nation, quoting from this poem:*

High Flight

*Oh, I have slipped the surly bonds of earth
And danced the skies on laughter-silvered wings;
Sunward I've climbed, and joined the tumbling mirth
Of sun-split clouds and done a hundred things
You have not dreamed of wheeled and soared and swung
High in the sunlit silence. Hov'ring there,
I've chased the shouting wind along, and flung
My eager craft through footless halls of air.
Up, up the long, delirious, burning blue
I've topped the windswept heights with easy grace
Where never lark, or even eagle flew
And, while with silent, lifting mind I've trod
The high untrespassed sanctity of space,
Put out my hand, and touched the face of God.*
—John Gillespie Magee, Jr. (killed in the Battle of Britain, age 19)

Ladies and gentlemen:

I'd planned to speak to you tonight to report on the state of the Union, but the events of earlier today have led me to change those plans. Today is a day for mourning and remembering. Nancy and I are pained to the core by the tragedy of the shuttle *Challenger*. We know we share this pain with all of the people of our country. This is truly a national loss.

Nineteen years ago, almost to the day, we lost three astronauts in a terrible accident on the ground. But we've never lost an astronaut in flight; we've never had a tragedy like this. And perhaps we've forgotten the courage it took for the crew of the shuttle. But they, the *Challenger* Seven, were aware of the dangers, but overcame them and did their jobs brilliantly. We mourn seven heroes: Michael Smith, Dick Scobee, Judith Resnik,

Ronald McNair, Ellison Onizuka, Gregory Jarvis, and Christa McAuliffe. We mourn their loss as a nation together. For the families of the seven, we cannot bear, as you do, the full impact of this tragedy. But we feel the loss, and we're thinking about you so very much. Your loved ones were daring and brave, and they had that special grace, that special spirit that says, "Give me a challenge, and I'll meet it with joy." They had a hunger to explore the universe and discover its truths. They wished to serve, and they did. They served all of us.

We've grown used to wonders in this century. It's hard to dazzle us. But for 25 years the United States space program has been doing just that. We've grown used to the idea of space, and perhaps we forget that we've only just begun. We're still pioneers. They, the members of the *Challenger* crew, were pioneers.

And I want to say something to the schoolchildren of America who were watching the live coverage of the shuttle's takeoff. I know it is hard to understand, but sometimes painful things like this happen. It's all part of the process of exploration and discovery. It's all part of taking a chance and expanding man's horizons. The future doesn't belong to the fainthearted; it belongs to the brave. The *Challenger* crew was pulling us into the future, and we'll continue to follow them.

I've always had great faith in and respect for our space program, and what happened today does nothing to diminish it. We don't hide our space program. We don't keep secrets and cover things up. We do it all up front and in public. That's the way freedom is, and we wouldn't change it for a minute. We'll continue our quest in space. There will be more shuttle flights and more shuttle crews and, yes, more volunteers, more civilians, more teachers in space. Nothing ends here; our hopes and our journeys continue. I want to add that I wish I could talk to every man and woman who works for NASA or who worked on this mission and tell them: Your dedication and professionalism have moved and impressed us for decades. And we know of your anguish. We share it.

There's a coincidence today. On this day 390 years ago, the great explorer Sir Francis Drake died aboard ship off the coast of Panama. In his lifetime, the great frontiers were the oceans, and an historian later said, "He lived by the sea, died on it, and was buried in it." Well, today we can say of the *Challenger* crew: Their dedication was, like Drake's, complete.

The crew of the space shuttle *Challenger* honored us by the manner in which they lived their lives. We will never forget them, nor the last time we saw them, this morning, as they pre-pared for their journey and waved goodbye, and "slipped the surly bonds of earth" to "touch the face of God."

Note: For links to some great online speech sites, see the Painless Speaking website at http://www.edreinvented.com/products/painless-speaking

APPENDIX C—MARKED TEXT

The three selections in Appendix C contain answers for Brain Ticklers 19, 20, and 21. Each demonstrates a way of marking a text for reading aloud. Because there is not a definitive way to mark text, you will not find a complete answer here. The sports essay and story each have two paragraphs marked. The scene from a play is the script belonging to the actress playing the part of Hannah and shows her score with her notes.

Dress for demonstrating exercises.

Visual aids: Slides=∿∿

underline=stress
/ = Breath or Pause

Golf Fitness: What You Don't Know Might Hurt You
by Dr. John J. Bisaccia,
Certified Sports Chiropractic Physician

For years golf was considered a game played by non-athletes and older individuals/ It seemed to lack the essentials of competition/ i.e./ fit athletes demonstrating skill and endurance/ while competing head-to-head in exciting matches for large sums of money/ However/ with the arrival of players such as Tiger Woods, the face of golf and the idea of a golfer as a non-athlete have changed drastically/ As if by some revelation/ professional golfers came to realize that being physically and aerobically fit could lead to longer drives/ more powerful iron shots/ and greater endurance/ while all along decreasing their chance of a career-ending injury/ These ideas have reached recreational golfers/ who have now started to work out in hopes of turning bogies into birdies/ While the potential for improving their game is enormous/ it must be done with sports-specific principles as opposed to generic workout routines/

The PGA recognizes physical fitness as one of the six basic aspects to the game of golf, to be given equal weight with equipment, basic instruction, advanced instruction, mental preparation, and course management. With that in mind, more and more amateur golfers are now taking advantage of sport-specific training towards golf in order to improve their own games and ward off or improve on injured areas. Injuries for amateur and professional golfers are very common. However, the two groups of golfers tend to have different areas that become injured. A right-handed professional will most likely suffer from left wrist pain, lower back pain, and left shoulder pain in that order, while a right-handed amateur golfer will most likely suffer from lower back pain, left elbow pain, and left shoulder pain, in that order. In fact, lower back injuries to amateur golfers constitute 53% of the injuries treated. So regardless of the level of play, the lower back appears to be the vulnerable site for injury.

Injuries to the lower back may be caused by a combination of factors, including faulty swing mechanics, poor flexibility, inadequate trunk strength, and overuse. The golf swing requires the spine to rotate, bend laterally, and extend, three motions that do not combine naturally. During a single round of golf, a player may swing the club between 200 and 300 times on average, including practice swings. Multiply that times rounds per year and driving range practice, and you can see why this repetitive action can lead to injury of the discs, muscles, and facet joints of the spine. In fact, research has demonstrated that amateur players generate greater stress on the lower back than professionals. The reasoning is that less than optimal swing mechanics equates to more damaging motions. "What we lack in quality we make up in quantity." Thus correct posture and proper conditioning plays a major role in the prevention of lower back injuries.

In analyzing many golfers' physical capabilities, some general conclusions can be drawn. Most male golfers suffer from inflexibility, especially of the hamstrings, hip flexors, and lower back muscles, while most women golfers suffer from lack of strength in the glutes, abdominals, and oblique regions. Although these two combinations are different in the realm of treatment and conditioning, both these physical weaknesses lend toward injury in the lower back region. In addressing the inflexibility component, stretches for the hamstrings, hip flexors, and mid to low back regions are as follows:

In addressing the strength of the glutes, abdominal, and oblique regions, the following exercises could be very helpful:

Lunges

Crunches

Bicycle kicks

Russian twist

Balance on one foot

Bench press/push ups

Flexibility of the hamstrings, spinal muscles, and hip flexors can be accomplished by the following:

Knee to chest

Double knee to chest

Rotational stretch

Hip flexor lunge

Hamstring

For stretching, hold each stretch for 30 seconds, 2 repetitions, 1 time a day. Do not bounce—hold a steady tension and remember to breathe.

For strength exercises, perform as many repetitions as possible till fatigued.

For balance exercises, maintain position for up to 2 minutes.

One aspect to note is that although a female golfer may not benefit as much from performing the stretching exercises, most male golfers would benefit from adding the strengthening exercises as well. If you have a lower back or other health problem that prohibits you from doing these exercises, please talk to a trained sports-specific professional to help you customize a program to fit your needs. Both men and women would benefit from at least 30 minutes of cardiovascular exercise (walking, biking, Stairmaster, etc.) four times a week to build endurance and heart health. This is very important, especially for a golfer who walks the course and finds himself/herself fatigued towards the 14th and 15th holes, barely having enough stamina to finish the 18th. Take a look at your scorecards and see how your performance declines as the golf day progresses.

Golf is a wonderful game that we can play throughout our life, especially into our elder years. Proper strength and conditioning can not only help you play better in the present moment, but can secure a future for you in this sport.

"An analogy is when 2 things are alike. The story I'm going to read to you has an analogy in it. See if you can figure out what 2 things are alike. The story is called:"

NELL'S KITTENS   AN ANALOGY

^ *by*   A.D. Laberge   *|| for pause*
= for stress

This big, old house has been a stagecoach inn. The house is nested into a <u>steep</u> hill. So steep is the hill that the *Contrast* (back door) is on level ground and the (front door) is very, <u>very</u> high up. Perhaps (once) there was a high porch. (Now) the old *Contrast* inn is mainly empty, except for Jon and Nell the cat. They are <u>good</u> <u>friends</u>. Nell often curls up on Jon's lap hoping to get rubbed behind the ears or gently stroked. Nell is a country *— Pause here* cat—small, gray, friendly, and clever.

DO <u>YOU</u> KNOW A NICE CAT?

Nell feeds herself. She's a <u>very</u> good hunter. <u>Country</u> cats eat mice, moles, birds, and <u>any</u> little creature they can catch. A cat's skill as a mouse catcher is <u>very</u> valuable, <u>especially</u> on a farm. Often Nell brings her supper home and surprises Jon. Jon//, being a person and not a cat//, sometimes is squeamish when he finds Nell's supper on the rug by their bed. But he understands that Nell is behaving <u>just</u> as a <u>cat</u> <u>should</u>.

WOULD YOU EAT DINNER ON A RUG?

→ *(That means that seeing Nell's dinner makes his tummy feel funny.)*

Jon notices that Nell's slender sides seem wider. For 63 days she grows wider and wider. Until one morning Jon hears sounds from his big, cardboard, laundry box. He looks into the box, and there is Nell with 3 tiny babies, as small or smaller than your hand. One is white, one is spotted, and the littlest is gray, just like Nell. The kittens can't walk—they mostly sleep. Their eyes are closed, and their ears are folded back. They can't hear or see yet.

HAVE YOU EVER TRIED TO SLEEP IN A CARDBOARD BOX?

Nell suckles her kittens until they are full of milk. Eating and sleeping helps them to grow. Jon leaves nutritious food and fresh water for Nell, near the big brown box. After 3 days, Nell leaves for a short time to hunt for her own food. As the kittens grow, Nell's trips away from the laundry box get longer.

Nell is a patient mother. Her kittens are busy growing and learning. Their eyes open after 12 days. They learn to use their legs just like children do. First they crawl, then they walk, and then they run. By the time the kittens are 35 days old, they are little scampering, stumbling balls of fluff. The kittens have learned to eat and drink and run and play. Jon loves to watch this silly stumbling circus of kittens. But soon the tiny acrobats huddle together and sleep—growing and playing takes lots of energy.

DO YOU THINK YOU GROW WHEN YOU SLEEP?

Nell knows a mother is a teacher. She speaks to her kittens with greeting, scolding, and warning sounds. She teaches by example. One day she brings back a very lifeless mouse. The kittens play & bat the small, gray morsel around, thinking it's a toy, not knowing that Nell is starting to teach them how to hunt.

DO YOU PLAY WITH YOUR FOOD?

As the kittens grow, Nell increases the challenge—each time the mouse is more and more lively. The final mouse is quick and healthy. Nell drops the mouse on the rug. It runs. The kittens run. The mouse is very fast—it runs away. The kittens are learning. They learn the smell of a mouse, the sound of a mouse, the quickness of a mouse, and the taste of mouse.

HOW COME CAT FOOD ISN'T LABELED "MOUSE" FLAVOR?

Next Nell brings her kittens outside, to the yard in front of the big, old house. Her tail is a flag they can follow. They play hide-go-seek, follow-the-leader, and stalking games in the tall grass. Play is the work of children and kittens—they learn as they play. Nell's kittens have a lot to learn before they can catch their own food and take care of themselves.

WOULD YOU LIKE TO BE A COUNTRY KITTEN?

An example of how an actor might score a script

(HANNAH'S SCRIPT)

A cutting taken from the play THE NEW SURVIVORS.* Scene Two. *Terezin—We Must Survive!* (pp. 13-17)

HANNAH   *"GRAB" THE FIRST LINE AND PLAY THESE ACTIONS FROM THE READING POSITION.*

(Lifting her head. Spots Darren.) Darren, wake up! Go stand guard! Tell us if anyone is coming.

> PLAYING A GAME AT NIGHT UNDER EXTREME DANGER WILL MAKE THE SITUATION MORE EXCITING, MORE THRILLING

(Darren gets up and looks out the side window.)   *STRESS THIS AS A LOUD STAGE WISPER.*

DARREN

No guards! I'll tell you if I see any.   *I CAN GIVE DARREN A THUMBS UP HERE.*

HANNAH

Emily, Sara, let's wake the others.   *PANTOMIME SHAKING EMILY & SARA WITH ONE HAND JUST GESTURING*

   "GRAB" ALL LINES

EMILY

(Still mostly asleep, she responds too loudly.) WHAT?

IF READING IN A CIRCLE - GRAB + MAKE EYE CONTACT WHEN APPROPRIATE
IF IN A LINE FACING AN AUDIENCE - GRAB + PRETEND TO MAKE EYE CONTACT BY PLAYING ALL LINES FORWARD

---

* Shell-scripting is a theatrical technique that allows me to use my craft as a professional theatre artist/educator to blend a successful and aesthetic script from the work of community or school participants (who may be actors or non-actors, but who are not theatre professionals) who come together to collaborate in creating social issue theatre specific to an existing community or school problem. *The New Survivors* is an excerpt from the result of a shell-scripting process in an elementary school fifth grade classroom confronting issues of violence after 9/11: They chose to address the issue by working with me to create a theatre piece exploring the Holocaust

—Xan Johnson

HANNAH

Shhh! You want to get us all killed?!!

> SUBTEXT: "I FEEL RESPONSIBLE."
>
> WITH A GESTURE
>
> LOOK BRIEFLY AT DARREN. ASK HIM TO GIVE A GESTURE THAT MEANS—"IT'S STILL OK."

EMILY

Sorry!

SARA

(Still mostly asleep and grabbing Emily's foot by mistake.) Hannah is that you?

> TRYING TO SUPPRESS MY OWN LAUGHTER AS I ENJOY MY TWO CLOSE FRIENDS

EMILY

(Retrieving her foot.) Sara, it's me, Emily! OK? And this is my FOOT, not Hannah.

SARA

Sorry, Em - mil - lee! (To Hannah.) Are we going to play the Animal Game?

> EYE + BODY EXPRESSIONS
>
> FLASH HER A LOOK.

HANNAH

Yes! Wake the others.

> AD LIB HERE.

(The three girls hurriedly wake everyone to play the Animal Game.)

EMILY

(Too loud.) HANNAH, CAN I GO FIRST!

INTERNAL DIALOGUE
"WHAT HAVE I DONE? WE'LL ALL GET CAUGHT."

HANNAH

WAVING AN ARM AT EMILY TO QUIET DOWN. I MIGHT LOOK AT DARREN TO GET THE OK TO CONTINUE

Shhhhh! Yes, but we've got to be quiet.

OVER ARTICULATE WITH LIPS

EMILY

Ok, I was alive in this millennium, but I'm extinct! (Emily begins her pantomime: the extinct Great Auk.)

INTERNAL DIALOGUE
"THAT'S A GOOD ONE EMILY"
I CAN'T HELP
BUT SMILING

PAVEL

That's easy, you're a duck!

ESPECIALLY ME,

(Laughter followed by lots of *shhhhh – ing!*)

EMILY

Ducks are still with us today, dah!

INTERNAL DIALOGUE
"I WOULDN'T HAVE KNOWN THAT ONE."

RUBIN

Oh, I know. You're a Great Auk.

EMILY

Yes. (To Pavel.) See, Pavel!

HANNAH

INTENTION: TO KEEP THE GAME MOVING AND TO AVOID CONFLICT. I AM RESPONSIBLE INTERNAL DIALOGUE.

Ok. You win a turn Rubin.

USE TO TAKE CONTROL. TAKE FOCUS.

RUBIN.

OK, I'm alive millions of years ago. (Rubin pantomimes being a Brontosaurus eating treetops.)

EMILY

You're a dinosaur!

PAVEL

Yes, but what kind?

EVA

AD LIB GESTURES THAT INDICATE I'M STILL KEEPING TRYING TO KEEP CONTROL AND QUIET. YET I EVERYONE. CANNOT HELP SMILING

A Tyrannosaurus Rex. (She pantomimes goofy viciousness.)

(Controlled laughter at Eva's goofy response.)

[handwritten:] ADLIBS CONTINUE

PAVEL

No.

(But, Eva continues her goofy performance until she gets the laugh she wants.)

RUTH

(Ruth has had enough.) Eva, it's eating the tops of trees. It must be a Brontosaurus.

PAVEL

Yes. Ruth's turn.

[handwritten:] BUT, I AM THE MOST ALERT IN PRETENDING TO SLEEP. I STAY READY

DARREN

(Shouting in a big whisper.) Gestapo!

(They all return to a sleeping position.)

[handwritten:] INTERNAL DIALOGUE: — "IT'S NOT YOUR TURN, ALEX." I GIVE HIM A DISAPPROVING LOOK.

They're passing by us. They went into another barracks. All clear.

ALEX

Hey, what am I? (He pantomimes being a Tyrannosaurus Rex.)

RUTH

(Still wanting a turn.) Rubin just did that one Alex. You're a Tyrannosaurus Rex.

ALEX

Wrong. I'm an EVA! (He jumps at Eva with a roar and begins to tickle her. (Eva screams) as others begin to tickle her also.)

I IMMEDIATELY BEGIN GESTURING TO QUIET THE FUN. I'M NOW WORRIED.

DARREN

GESTAPO! (All freeze.) They're headed for the train.

I VISUALIZE THE SCENE AS I STARE FORWARD, NOT MOVING, MY BODY RIGID. MY INTERNAL DIALOGUE: "THIS WILL BE US ONE DAY SOON."

(All the children gather and look out over the audience.)

DAVID

Look! It's those poor children from Poland. Must be over a thousand of them.

ALENA

They were part of that uprising against the Nazis in their Polish ghetto.

NINA

They've only been here a couple weeks. *TEARS FILL MY EYES*

273

ALENA

All trains heading that way go to Auschwitz from here. (MY EYES SHUT.)

NINA

Gas chamber.

ALL

(Quietly with felt meaning.) Gas chamber.

MY EYES OPEN
JUST BEFORE
I SPEAK

MY FACE DISTORTS INTO A FULL,
GENUINE SILENT SOB. I REPEAT
THIS THOUGHT OVER + OVER
IN MY MIND — "WE MUST SURVIVE!"
MY BOTTOM LIP STRENGTHENS.

HOLD UNTIL LIGHTS FADE
TO BLACK

GLOSSARY

ad lib (from *ad libitum*—in accordance with desire) to improvise lines or actions

gesture a movement that reveals the character's intention, spontaneous reaction, or specific communication; in theatre, all gesture must have meaning

give and take focus to purposely stop the flow of action and refocus attention; bring focus to one's self or pass it on

grab a line when reading dialogue from a script, read ahead to get the line in your head so that you can look up (interact realistically) to deliver it

intention what the character intends to do in one *beat*; each beat is a unit of action which taken all together make up the character's *super-objective* (the character's main objective that motivates a character throughout the entire play); thus intentions and beats are not separate and fragmented but only useful, working subdivisions of what is, and must appear as, a coherent whole (since dramatic unity requires that everything must interrelate)

internal dialogue when we are just shy of one year old as children, we begin a conversation with ourself inside our brain that cannot be stopped until we die or experience brain trauma

pantomime to convey with body and facial movements and no words

play all lines forward deliver lines facing the audience, not to the other actors

scoring a script preparing a script for a production by marking all of the important information that is needed on it; a script may be scored by an individual actor, by the director, or by the stage manager, each score reflecting the material for which that person is responsible

stage whisper a loud whisper that is meant to be audible to the audience but within the world of the play is accepted as having the carry of a normal whisper

subtext what the character is really feeling or thinking beneath the spoken text and action of a play

INDEX

Really. This isn't going to hurt at all . . .

Learning won't hurt when middle school and high school students open any *Painless* title. These books transform subjects into fun—emphasizing a touch of humor and entertaining brain-tickler puzzles that are fun to solve.

Extra bonus—each title followed by (*) comes with a FREE app!
Download a fun-to-play arcade game to your iPhone, iTouch, iPad, or Android™ device. The games reinforce the study material in each book and provide hours of extra fun.

Each book: Paperback

Painless Algebra, 3rd Ed.*
Lynette Long, Ph.D.
ISBN 978-0-7641-4715-9, $9.99, Can$11.99

Painless American Government
Jeffrey Strausser
ISBN 978-0-7641-2601-7, $9.99, Can$11.99

Painless American History, 2nd Ed.
Curt Lader
ISBN 978-0-7641-4231-4, $9.99, Can$11.99

Painless Chemistry*
Loris Chen
ISBN 978-0-7641-4602-2, $9.99, Can$11.99

Painless Earth Science*
Edward J. Denecke, Jr.
ISBN 978-0-7641-4601-5, $9.99, Can$11.99

Painless English for Speakers of Other Languages, 2nd Ed.*
Jeffrey Strausser and José Paniza
ISBN 978-1-4380-0002-2, $9.99, Can$11.50

Painless Fractions, 3rd Ed.*
Alyece Cummings, M.A.
ISBN 978-1-4380-0000-8, $9.99, Can$11.50

Painless French, 2nd Ed.*
Carol Chaitkin, M.S., and Lynn Gore, M.A.
ISBN 978-0-7641-4762-3, $9.99, Can$11.50

Painless Geometry, 2nd Ed.
Lynette Long, Ph.D.
ISBN 978-0-7641-4230-7, $9.99, Can$11.99

Painless Grammar, 3rd Ed.*
Rebecca S. Elliott, Ph.D.
ISBN 978-0-7641-4712-8, $9.99, Can$11.99

Painless Italian, 2nd Ed.*
Marcel Danesi, Ph.D.
ISBN 978-0-7641-4761-6, $9.99, Can$11.50

Painless Math Word Problems, 2nd Ed.
Marcie Abramson, B.S., Ed.M.
ISBN 978-0-7641-4335-9, $9.99, Can$11.99

Painless Poetry, 2nd Ed.
Mary Elizabeth
ISBN 978-0-7641-4591-9, $9.99, Can$11.99

Painless Pre-Algebra
Amy Stahl
ISBN 978-0-7641-4588-9, $9.99, Can$11.99

Painless Reading Comprehension, 2nd Ed.*
Darolyn E. Jones, Ed.D.
ISBN 978-0-7641-4763-0, $9.99, Can$11.50

Painless Spanish, 2nd Ed.*
Carlos B. Vega
ISBN 978-0-7641-4711-1, $9.99, Can$11.99

Painless Speaking, 2nd Ed.*
Mary Elizabeth
ISBN 978-1-4380-0003-9, $9.99, Can$11.50

Painless Spelling, 3rd Ed.*
Mary Elizabeth
ISBN 978-0-7641-4713-5, $9.99, Can$11.99

Painless Study Techniques
Michael Greenberg
ISBN 978-0-7641-4059-4, $9.99, Can$11.99

Painless Vocabulary, 2nd Ed.*
Michael Greenberg
ISBN 978-0-7641-4714-2, $9.99, Can$11.99

Painless Writing, 2nd Ed.
Jeffrey Strausser
ISBN 978-0-7641-4234-5, $9.99, Can$11.99

Barron's Educational Series, Inc.
250 Wireless Blvd.
Hauppauge, N.Y. 11788
Order toll-free: 1-800-645-3476
In Canada:
Georgetown Book Warehouse
34 Armstrong Ave.
Georgetown, Ontario L7G 4R9
Canadian orders: 1-800-247-7160

Prices subject to change without notice.

———To order———
Available at your local book store
or visit **www.barronseduc.com**

GRAMMAR GRAMMAR & MORE GRAMMAR

For ESL courses . . . for remedial English courses . . . for standard instruction in English grammar and usage on all levels from elementary through college . . . Barron's has what you're looking for!

501 English Verbs, 2nd Ed., w/CD-ROM
Thomas R. Beyer, Jr., Ph.D.
An analysis of English verb construction precedes 501 regular and irregular verbs presented alphabetically, one per page, each set up in table form showing indicative, imperative, and subjunctive moods in all tenses.
ISBN 978-0-7641-7985-3, paper, $18.99, Can$22.99

Grammar in Plain English, 5th Ed.
H. Diamond, M.A., and P. Dutwin, M.A.
Basic rules of grammar and examples clearly presented, with exercises that reflect GED test standards.
ISBN 978-0-7641-4786-9, paper, $14.99, Can$16.99

Painless Grammar, 3rd Ed.
Rebecca Elliott, Ph.D.
Focused mainly toward middle-school students, this book takes a light, often humorous approach to teaching grammar and usage.
ISBN 978-0-7641-4712-8, paper, $9.99, Can$11.99

A Dictionary of American Idioms, 4th Ed.
A. Makkai, M. Boatner, and J. Gates
More than 8,000 American idioms and slang expressions are defined and explained.
ISBN 978-0-7641-1982-8, paper, $16.99, Can$19.99

E-Z Grammar, 2nd Ed.
Dan Mulvey
Barron's *E-Z Grammar* is written primarily for high school seniors and college freshmen and emphasizes the simple logic underlying correct grammar and clear expression. The author covers all parts of speech and correct sentence structure.
ISBN 978-0-7641-4261-1, paper, $14.99, Can$16.99

——————— To order ———————
Available at your local book store
or visit **www.barronseduc.com**

Barron's Educational Series, Inc.
250 Wireless Blvd.
Hauppauge, NY 11788
Order toll-free: 1-800-645-3476
Order by fax: 1-631-434-3217

In Canada:
Georgetown Book Warehouse
34 Armstrong Ave., Georgetown, Ont. L7G 4R9
Canadian orders: 1-800-247-7160
Fax in Canada: 1-800-887-1594

Prices subject to change without notice.

(#90) R 4/12